A READER'S GUIDE TO
RATIONAL EXPECTATIONS

£39-95

Appropriateness of assumptions of rational expectations.

Does new classical economics provide a convincing rationale for minimalist gov-

A Reader's Guide to Rational Expectations

A Survey and Comprehensive Annotated Bibliography

Deborah A. Redman

Tübingen University

Edward Elgar

Published by
Edward Elgar Publishing Limited
Gower House
Croft Road
Aldershot
Hants GU11 3HR
England

Edward Elgar Publishing Limited
Distributed in the United States by
Ashgate Publishing Company
Old Post Road
Brookfield
Vermont 05036
USA

A CIP catalogue record for this book is available from the British Library

Library of Congress Cataloging-in-Publication Data
Redman, Deborah A.
    A reader's guide to rational expectations: a survey and
comprehensive annotated bibliography/by Deborah A. Redman.
        p.   cm.
    1. Rational expectations (Economic theory) 2. Rational
expectations (Economic theory)–Bibliography. I. Title.
HB199.R43   1992
330'.01–dc20   91–34832
                                                              CIP

ISBN 1 85278 567 5   1673187

Printed in Great Britain by
Billing & Sons Ltd, Worcester

Contents

Foreword

Frank Hahn has written that 'economics is a subject in which the ambitious young had better be up to date with the latest fashion' (1983, p. 924). The major purpose of this work is to make staying up to date with rational expectations easier for economists in government, academia and industry, as well as for students.

In writing this work I wanted to provide the reader with an introduction to rational expectations which enables him or her to tackle the literature. That is the task of Part I. In Part II an annotated bibliography of the literature on rational expectations – which has reached a voluminous level in the 1980s – is put at the reader's fingertips. In the introduction to rational expectations (RE), I attempt the unattempted: to define the various versions of RE *verbally and formally* side by side so that the reader can immediately recognize that some definitions of RE are more restrictive than others. I have tried to hold the technical demands on the reader to a minimum and to use the clearest possible mathematical formulation of concepts and equations. Even the layman with a minimal knowledge of statistics and economics should be able to understand the text. The application of RE to microeconomics has not been included because the material is too technical to summarize gracefully and intelligibly.

Just as in Pesaran's admirable book of 1987, considerable space has been devoted here to discussing the limits of rational expectations, especially of the narrow version. Like Pesaran, Turnovsky (1984) and others, I conclude that the narrow version of RE is simply too restrictive to be useful in most macroeconomic models.

References to works in the bibliography appear in parentheses followed by the date. If the reference is to a book, the word 'book' appears to distinguish it from an article, e.g., (Pesaran, 1987: book) unless this is self-evident. The annotated bibliography in Part II contains 476 entries, of which 34 are books. Although the bibliography can not claim to be exhaustive, I nonetheless made an effort to be as comprehensive as possible. I searched the *Journal of Economic Literature* from 1969 to 1989 and *The Index of Economic Articles* for the years 1961 to 1968 (before the *JEL* was founded) under 'macroeconomic theory, general' (023) and 'microeconomic theory, general' (022). But in order for a work to find its way into this bibliography, the title had to suggest that RE were being used or discussed. The substance of the article or book had to deal directly with

RE to be included. No doubt some works which deal chiefly with RE have been omitted because their titles did not alert me to their content. By checking the bibliographies of the works already listed, I was able to incorporate a number of neglected sources. An exhaustive bibliography, however, would require a manual search of the journals.

In researching the work and compiling the bibliography I benefited from, and extend my thanks for, the gracious hospitality of numerous librarians at the University of Bielefeld and Tübingen University.

Acknowledgements

The author gratefully acknowledges permission to reproduce parts of the following sources:

Donald M. McCloskey (1985), *The Rhetoric of Economics*, Madison, Wisconsin: University of Wisconsin Press, for the table on p. 6; by permission of the University of Wisconsin Press.

Leslie T. Oxley (1983), 'Rational Expectations and Macroeconomic Policy: A Review Article', *Scottish Journal of Political Economy*, **30** (2), June, for the graph on p. 20; by permission of the *Scottish Journal of Political Economy*.

Categorizing the rational expectations literature annotated in Part II (by entry number)*

Originators of the concept of RE

332	354	463

Surveys and reviews (r) of RE

1	127	261
2	128(r)	269(r)
6	130	295
7	155	297
11	168	299
22	174	303
29	179	313
30	192	366(r)
31	194	374
32	200	403
56	205(r)	416
62	206	419
68	227	424
74	228(r)	428
107	238	452
114	240	

Works of the new classical economists

2	28	202
17	29	274–94
18	62–7	306–22
19	201	403–11

On RE and Keynes/Keynesian economics

54	264	393
70	265	399
101	273	415
156	282	436
260	294	472

*Not all of the entries appearing in the bibliography fall into one of these categories.

Criticisms of and insights into the new classical economics

Corrections of mistakes

Econometric aspects of RE models

On the policy neutrality result

7	156	315
8	163	316
10	164	317
14	165	322
15	182	324
21	199	333
35	218	339
40	220	365
49	222	380
53	225	389
71	227	390
72	229	392
116	231	426
117	245	429
141	246	437
142	302	444
143	309	467
144	312	476
145	314	

On solving RE models

17	110	230
19	132	268
34	180	308
52	183	336
81	207	369
83	208	413
84	209	442
99	210	458
100	212	459
103		

Expanding/building on the RE concept and models

37	189	335
47	195	337
48	196	338
55	197	344
58	203	345
59	213	346
72	215	347
75	216	351
76	219	353
77	222	356
78	223	359
79	232	361
88	237	363
89	239	367
105	242	368
108	243	370
111	248	371
112	250	372
113	251	379
117	252	381
120	267	382
125	271	385
132	274	391
139	288	398
147	300	418
148	305	446
149	306	449
154	307	450
157	310	453
169	321	454
170	328	461
171	329	465
175	330	474
186	331	

PART I

A READER'S GUIDE TO RATIONAL EXPECTATIONS

1 Introduction

The purpose of this introduction to rational expectations (RE) is not to survey all of the existing literature of and on the rational expectations school. The present, more limited, aim is to achieve the following:

1. to examine in a nontechnical way what it means to form expectations of economic variables rationally;
2. to show in what ways the concept itself is ambiguous – perhaps the most salient feature of the rational expectations school. It is well worth stressing, even by way of introduction, that

   > [r]ational expectations is not an unambiguous concept. There exist almost as many versions as there are members of the school, and later versions of the same author often are different from, and more qualified than, earlier ones (Haberler, 1980(b), p. 274);

3. to represent criticisms of the school from all theoretical corners of the discipline;
4. to discuss the evolution of the concept and its implications for stabilization policy;
5. to review briefly the empirical findings concerning RE; and
6. to put the school into perspective within the broader scope of general economics.

An approach to rational expectations cannot be that of the historian of economic analysis who knows the ultimate fate of the movement (such as that of adaptive expectations). Since we do not know how these views ultimately will fare, it would be inappropriate to attempt to reach a definitive assessment of the school. What can be done, however, is to present summaries of the views within the school and some of the important objections raised against them. The extent to which such criticisms and objections are damaging to the movement is a matter of current debate which cannot be fully resolved here. However, this introduction can provide a perspective for understanding these controversies and for focusing more sharply on theoretical and empirical problems which need to be addressed or rectified.

Certainly the development of RE, which Begg (1982) claims has 'revolutionized macroeconomics', deserves to be understood as a diverse and evolving school of thought still in transition. The first step towards under-

standing is to grasp what the concept means. That is the focus of the first
section where three versions of RE are defined and explained: Muth's
formulation of rational expectations, a narrower version which modifies
Muth's definition for applications in macroeconomics, and a generalized
version of rational expectations. The second step towards understanding
is to recognize the shortcomings and limitations of a concept, keeping in
mind Gunnar Myrdal's astute observation that ignorance and knowledge
both tend to be opportunist.[1] Thereafter, the following topics are discussed: criticisms of the narrow version of rational expectations, stabilization policy and the new classical school, the natural rate hypothesis
(NRH) in new classical models, the embodiment of the rational expectations hypothesis (REH) in non-market-clearing and market-clearing
models, and the empirical evidence for and against the REH.

2 Defining rational expectations

Mr. Muth and the origins

John Muth first introduced the concept of RE to economists in his article 'Rational Expectations and the Theory of Price Movements', published in *Econometrica* in 1961. At approximately the same time, Edwin S. Mills (1957 and 1962) introduced the very similar concept of 'implicit expectations' – the idea that future values can be proxies for expectations because economic agents forecast correctly and errors remain small (see also Lovell, 1986).

What helped to bring the school to the forefront was a growing dissatisfaction with the state of macroeconomic theory and with its record of demand-management policies in controlling unemployment and inflation. The Phillips curve relationship floundered in the 1970s as inflation and unemployment rose simultaneously; the Keynesian theoretical machinery also failed to incorporate inflation-rate expectations into Keynesian models to explain the problem. D.F. Gordon describes the situation thus:

> [W]ithout an economic explanation of the Phillips curve we simply have no theory of employment and unemployment and of movements of aggregate output and the price level in the short run.[2]

One of the reasons for the rapid adoption of RE was its emphasis on an existing weakness in economic modelling; that is, the *ad hoc* specification of models of expectations. But without doubt the main reason for RE's sudden popularity was the startling new classical policy neutrality results, which generated a tremendous literature. Donald McCloskey has prepared a table of the citations of Muth's 1961 article before and after the policy neutrality conclusion of the new classical economists was published (from 1966–82). McCloskey's table, updated to 1987, is reproduced below.[3]

Annual Citations of Muth's Article (1966–82)

1966	5	1974	10	1981	56
1967	3	1975	20	1982	74
1968	2	1976	33	1983	63
1969	2	1977	44	1984	75
1970	4	1978	47	1985	59
1971	2	1979	44	1986	52
1972	9	1980	71	1987	44
1973	10				

Source: Social Science Citation Index. The index begins in 1966.

Clearly there was a '1980's boom' in citations after the new classical results were published. Two other related trends accompanied the rise to prominence of the RE school: (1) the greater acceptance of monetarist ideas, and (2) the search for microeconomic foundations for macro-economic theory and the subsequent spurning of the non-market-clearing approach.

The intellectual origins of the rational expectations hypothesis reach back to a 1954 paper by Grunberg and Modigliani in which they argue that individuals reacting to the published prediction of a future event will not necessarily influence the course of that event and thereby falsify the prediction.[4] This result allows social scientists some margin for error in their public predictions. Six year later, Herbert Simon, Franco Modig-liani, John Muth and Charles Holt collaborated on a work dealing with inventory management and production control of the theory of the firm, the goal being to define operational rules given uncertainty.[5] In this paper the authors assume that 'certainty equivalents' exist for the values to be predicted. Certainly equivalence is a property of linear RE models: a random model is said to exhibit certainty equivalence if the solution of a stochastic model differs from that of a deterministic (nonrandom) model only in the sense that actual values of future variables are replaced by current expectations of these future variables.

In this paper by Simon, Modigliani, Muth and Holt, two assumptions were made which would cause a model to exhibit 'certainty equivalence': (1) the cost functions were assumed to be quadratic, and (2) firms only needed to consider the expected value of future sales. Simon cautioned that the certainty equivalence property did not characterize economic behaviour in general, but was useful in restricted situations. John Muth (1961, p. 316), on the other hand, extended the concept's emphasis on expected values, linking expectations to the relevant economic theory and to reality:

I should like to suggest that expectations, since they are informed predictions of future events, are essentially the same as the predictions of the relevant economic theory. At the risk of confusing this purely descriptive hypothesis with a pronouncement as to what firms ought to do, we call such expectations 'rational'. It is sometimes argued that the assumption of rationality in economics leads to theories inconsistent with, or inadequate to explain, observed phenomena, especially changes over time .... . Our hypothesis is based on exactly the opposite point of view: that dynamic economic models do not assume enough rationality.

The hypothesis can be rephrased a little more precisely as follows: that expectations of firms (or, more generally, the subjective probability distribution of outcomes) tend to be distributed, for the same information set, about the prediction of the theory (or the 'objective' probability distributions of outcomes).

Thus we have arrived at our first definition of RE:

Definition 1: Muth's Version of Rational Expectations
Expectations can be represented by the subjective probability distribution and tend to be distributed about the prediction of the theory, that is, about the objective probability distribution of outcomes. In other words, the weighted arithmetic mean of the expectations is equal to the prediction of the relevant economic model. The expected values of the variable to be forecast and the actual variables of the variable *have a common mean value*.

Muth's definition of RE leaves considerable room for qualification. For instance, he refers to 'a subjective probability distribution' but to ' "objective" probability distributions'. Why is there only one subjective, but multiple objective distributions? Are the objective distributions from one model or from numerous models (Colander and Guthrie, 1980–81, p. 221)? Why is 'objective' enclosed in quotation marks?

Muth applied the concept to microeconomics – specifically to the cobweb model as it related to agricultural markets. His model was linear; almost all RE models are linear (often log linear). Rational expectations are generated from a reduced form equation or set of equations. Individuals understand (or have enough information to understand) the structural parameters of the model as well as the systematic components of government's fiscal and monetary policy from which they can then determine the stochastic processes which generate the exogenous variables. Muth contends that people's subjective expectations are, on average, equal to the true values of the variable (which means that forecasts are on average correct). The beauty of using RE is that agents do not make systematic forecasting errors.

Muth's definition modified: the carry-over to macroeconomics
Business Week ('How Expectations Defeat Economic Policy', 1976) opened its report on the macroeconomic version of RE in this way:

> A controversial new theory called rational expectations is sweeping through the economics profession. It says that economic policy is impotent. Systematic policy changes can do little to increase employment and output, because the public – individuals and institutions – takes actions that offset the changes.

This is *not* a definition of RE, but a description of the early policy conclusions of the new classical school. The extensive confusion of policy conclusions obtained from new classical RE models with the hypothesis itself has led to unwarranted criticism of the REH.

The REH was first applied to macroeconomics as 'consistent expectations' by A. A. Walters in a little-known paper published in 1971, and by Lucas (1972 and 1977) and Sargent and Wallace (1975) a few years later. The Minnesota group's definition 'went well beyond that of a Bayesian predictor derived from explicit optimizing behavior' (Buiter, 1980, p. 34). Muth's definition was first extended by Lucas and Prescott who contended (1971, p. 660) that they were modelling expectations to the 'opposite extreme' of adaptive expectations. They called price expectations rational when the subjective probability distribution of future economic variables held at time t coincided with the actual, objective conditional distribution based on all the information assumed to be available at time t. We shall call this the narrow version of RE and define it formally in the following way.

Definition 2: Narrow Version of Rational Expectations
Subjective expectations held by economic agents are the same as the conditional mathematical expectations of the true probability model of the economy. In other words, agents' subjective probability distributions coincide with the objective probability distribution of events. Then the expected values of the variable to be forecast and the actual values *have the same probability distribution.*

Muth's definition was thus modified so that behaviour over time depended not on the central tendency, but on the subjective probability distribution held by economic agents. The Lucas-Prescott definition of RE requires that the subjective distribution (and not its mean) be exactly equal to the true conditional distribution based on all available information at time t. In statistical notation, the REH takes the form

$$_{t-1}X_t^e \equiv E(X_t / I_{t-1})$$

where $_{t-1}X_t^e$ is the subjective expected value of variable X (in other words, the value of variable X at time t which is expected by individuals forming expectations in period $t-1$), and $E(X_t/I_{t-1})$ is the conditional expected value of X_t given (conditional on) the set of total information available at time $t-1$, I_{t-1}. $E(X_t/I_{t-1})$ is an unbiased predictor of X_t.

The forecast error, $\epsilon = X_t - E(X_t/I_{t-1})$, has two essential properties. First, the conditional expectation of the forecast error is zero; that is, $E(\epsilon_t / I_{t-1}) = 0$. Second, it is serially uncorrelated with information available to agents, given a one-period forecast horizon. (It does not hold, for instance, if agents form expectations about the value of X for two periods ahead.) In other words, it is a white-noise error term. This second characteristic is called the error orthogonality property. If the forecast error did not possess this property, agents could improve their forecast by incorporating new information into it. The orthogonality property ensures that forecast errors are unpredictable and thus unrelated to information available at the time of the forecast. Expectations diverge from actual values of the variable forecasted because of unpredictable elements.

Generalized to $t+k$ periods, we have the RE of X formed at time t for the variable X at time $t+k$:

$$_{t+k}X_t^e \equiv E(X_{t+k} / I_t), k > 0$$

where $_{t+k}X_t^e$ is the forecast of X formed at time t for time $t+k$.

It must be stressed, however, that the RE of a variable is not *at all times* the expected (or mean) value of the variable based on all available information; there has been some confusion in the literature about this (see McDonald, 1987). Likewise, RE do not imply perfect foresight: if there were no uncertainty, rational expectations would then coincide with perfect foresight. But since perfect foresight and certainty do not characterize the economic environment, they must be addressed. It is thus natural to query what amount of information individuals should be assumed to possess, how much is assumed to be available at no cost, and how agents learn. These questions, left open by Muth and the narrow version of RE, led to yet another more general definition.

But before we proceed to this generalized definition of RE, it is necessary to mention the Lucas critique. During the 1970s when the Phillips curve broke down and 'stagflation' was coined, the predictive power of the large macroeconometric models also faltered. With the advent of the RE movement, it became clear that one problem was the assumption of constant structural parameters underlying the models. It was Lucas who showed how RE can have a major impact on the policy evaluation of econometric macroeconomic models.

Corollary: The Lucas Critique
If expectations are assumed to be rational, economic agents adjust their expectations when government policy changes. Macroeconomic models should thus take into account the fact that any change in policy will systematically alter the structure of the econometric model. Because the estimated equations in most existing macroeconomic models do not change with alternative policies, the advice from model simulations could be misleading. The Lucas critique implies that the building of macroeconometric models needs to be wholly reconsidered so that the equations are structural or behavioural in nature.

The generalized version of rational expectations
The generalized version of rational expectations grew out of criticisms of the narrow version. The basic notion is that individuals form expectations optimally on the basis of all the information available to them and on the costs of using that information, that is, to the point where the marginal cost of gathering information equals its marginal benefit.

Definition 3: Weak Version of Rational Expectations
Rational agents form expectations by acquiring and using information to the point where the expected marginal cost and the expected marginal benefit of gathering and using this information are equal.

This definition has two major drawbacks: first, it lacks operational significance and, second, expectations are not necessarily free from systematic
error. Since the two previous versions of RE ignore the costs of infor-
mation-gathering, they are often called the 'all-information' or 'global
information' approaches. Because the adjective 'rational' in economics is
generally reserved to describe the outcome of a utility maximization
process, and since the other two definitions of RE are rational only when
the marginal cost of gathering information equals zero, one could argue
with Maddock and Carter (1982) that it may be more useful to refer to the
general version as *rational* expectations (with the emphasis on rational)
and to rename the other two versions. Colander and Guthrie (1980–81, p.
219) offer the term 'reasonable expectations'.[6] In the end, however, the
breakdown into the Muth, the narrow and the generalized versions of the
REH seems to be the least confusing taxonomy. It also has the advantage
of reminding the reader that RE has undergone a considerable evolution
in its first 30 years of existence.

The generalized version has not dominated the literature to date, but
according to David Begg (1982: book) and Stanley Fischer (1980: book, p.
212), it will do so in the future. Most consistent with neoclassical economics, this version allows for an infinite variety of specifications because
no consensus has been reached on how much information is optimal or
realistic for agents to collect. Hence the definition of RE in the generalized
form becomes model-dependent.

It is worth mentioning that some authors have drawn a distinction
between adaptive (sometimes referred to as backwards-looking) and
rational (sometimes called forward-looking) expectations in order to
emphasize the rationality of the narrow version. This distinction, however, is too simplistic, as William Poole (1976, p. 483, n. 27) so clearly
explains in the passage below:

> . . . Muth showed how adaptive expectations could be rational under certain
> assumptions as to the stochastic structure of the market if the adaptive param-
> eter reflected the structure. However, it remains true that adaptive expectations
> are not rational if other information besides the past behavior of a variable can
> improve predictions.

Finally, we must sound a word of warning to the reader. The version
most frequently encountered in the earlier literature is a form of the
narrow and not the generalized version. The reader investigating RE will
be confronted with a multifarious nomenclature: rational expectations,
the strong version, the strict form, the global or all-information approach
are all used to designate either Muth's RE or the narrow version. The

generalized version is often referred to as the weak form, the mild version, the diluted version, economically rational expectations or *rational* expectations. But often the reader will encounter 'rational expectations' without further qualification. The categories presented here are aimed at minimizing the confusion that could result from such multiple nomenclature.

3 Critique of the narrow version of rational expectations

Most criticisms have been aimed at the narrow version of RE,[7] a great number at the information availability assumption, together with other important but unrelated objections.

Objections challenging the validity of the information availability assumption
Benjamin Friedman (1979, pp. 25–6) most aptly captures the essence of early misunderstandings of the narrow version of the REH:

> Much of the confusion surrounding the meaning of 'rational' expectations is due to a failure to distinguish between (a) the general assumption that economic agents use efficiently whatever information is available and (b) a specific assumption identifying the available set of information.
>
> The *information exploitation* assumption (a), which Muth (1961, pp. 315–16) clearly identified as a part of his 'rational expectations hypothesis', can hardly seem objectionable. In its broadest construction it simply states, as a condition for optimizing behavior, that people exploit information until the point at which its marginal product equals its (perhaps zero) marginal cost.
>
> The specific *information availability* assumption (b) in Muth's 'rational expectations hypothesis' is that the information which is available to economic agents is sufficient to permit them to form expectations characterized by conditional subjective distributions of outcomes indicated by 'the relevant economic theory'. In other words, people not only observe or know in advance the values of certain economic variables but also draw, on the basis of those known values, inferences which are identical to the inferences of the process actually generating the outcomes in question. People form their expectations as if they know, to within a set of additive white-noise disturbances, the structure of the economic process itself.

With this framework in mind, let us examine more closely the conceptual difficulties which the two narrower versions have encountered.

In those cases in which the costs of acquiring information are positive, both narrower versions of RE are inconsistent with the assumptions of utility maximization for the consumer and profit maximization for the firm. Feige and Pearce (1976) construct a model which takes into account the costs of acquiring information and call the result 'economically rational expectations'. But as Robert Shiller (1978, p. 35) concludes: 'Once we do this, we can no longer equate "rationality" with the assumption that market expectations are true mathematical expectations conditioned on

13

all information.' This brings us back to the generalized version of the REH.

It has been argued that since agents must possess knowledge of the complete model of the economy, the narrow version of RE is an unrealistic assumption, inconsistent with optimal information models. Hahn has described the power of the assumption as substituting 'an internal and psychic hand for the market. Each individual somehow has learned how the invisible (hand) would have performed if it had been given markets in which to perform.'[8] Pesaran argues that the 'as if' version of RE is fallacious and that the properties of unbiasedness and orthogonality have been misunderstood.

> [F]or rational expectations to have the desired (statistical) properties of unbiasedness and orthogonality it is not enough, as is often stated by some authors, that individuals form expectations 'as if' they knew the 'true' model of the economy. They should actually know the 'true' model, or else they should be capable of learning what the 'true' model is, given their *a priori* beliefs and the past history of the economy (1987: book, p. 2).

The two narrower versions are inconsistent with learning models of behaviour. If a learning process is incorporated into the model, the generalized version of the REH is probably being employed. Benjamin Friedman (1979) introduces optimal learning by a least-squares procedure which is consistent with rationality in a Rawlsian sense: 'the rationality of a person's choice does not depend upon how much he knows, but upon how well he reasons from whatever information he has, however incomplete.'[9] Cyert and DeGroot (1974) introduce a Bayesian learning procedure into a RE framework and conclude that it is consistent with a Bayesian framework. Also incorporating a learning process into his model, Stephen DeCanio concludes that economical use of information will not generally generate a narrow version of RE:

> The only general statement that can be made about rationality in expectation formation is that maximizing behavior will lead to forecasting methods that depend on the cost of information, the intrinsic difficulty of the forecasting problem, and the benefits to be obtained from accurate predictions (DeCanio, 1979, p. 55).

Pesaran (1987: book, p. 3) analyses problems with the learning process assumed within a RE framework:

> When information is costly the problem of learning becomes much more complicated. First, the decision to collect information, and hence the possibility of learning, can be stifled by agents' *a priori* held subjective beliefs. Second, when information is costly it may not be worthwhile to learn the 'true' model

even if it were in fact possible to do so. Thus, in the face of costly information, contrary to what is predicted by the Muth version of the REH, there is no ground for believing that 'rational' optimizing agents will necessarily form expectations that are free of systematic errors.

The narrow version of RE does not provide a theory of how expectations are formed. The issue of how economic agents acquire their knowledge of the true structure of the economy in order to make forecasts is not addressed by the theory (B. Friedman, 1979; Anderson and Sonnenschein, 1985).

The implication is that the transition problem to the narrow RE equilibrium is assumed away; thus the kind of factors which allow for a distinction between the long and short run dissipate. The information availability assumption and the neglect of expectation formation place these models in a long-run equilibrium context (Buiter, 1980) in which, first, capital in the neoclassical sense is meaningless because the long-run rate of profit falls to zero[10] (Colander and Guthrie, 1980–81, p. 219) and, second, the interest rate equals market time preference. For this reason 'it seems reasonable to view strict Muth-rational expectations as an acceptable representation of private (and public) agents' forecasting behavior only in the tranquillity of a long-run steady-state equilibrium' (Buiter, 1980, p. 38).

The models are inconsistent with observed patterns of expectations. Economists expect agents to possess generalized knowledge. Arrow contends that, on the contrary, agents have specialized knowledge; there is no reason why individual forecasts should be based on the general kind of information an econometrician would use.[11] Forecasts will be based on *more* information than is contained in econometric models since individuals base their expectations on all the information at their disposal, which may include sources not available to others. Likewise, individuals will not use all information contained in an econometric model; they concentrate on what is most useful and exclude the rest.[12] The implications for this are (1) that expectations embedded in any model may not be the best forecast of that model; (2) that expectations of different agents may not be based on the same model; and (3) that expectations are not necessarily similar to one another (Katona, 1980; Struthers, 1984, p. 1139).

In the same paper, Struthers takes the argument one step further by broaching the subject of self-interest: why expect agents to share information? Evidence is to the contrary and suggests that even incentives will not guarantee that sufficient information is gathered to prevent systematic errors from occurring.

According to Paul Davidson (1982–83), agents relying on the narrow version of RE may even err when making crucial decisions. Noncrucial decisions involving small, noncostly differences in outcomes may be compatible with ergodic processes – those in which every sizeable sample is equally representative of the whole, as with respect to a statistical parameter – and hence with a narrow version of RE. But expensive, important decisions are not generally replicated and cannot be represented by the ergodic process. He argues that economic processes are inherently nonergodic. In the same article (pp. 191–2), Davidson enumerates four conditions which the narrow version would have to meet to act as a useful analogy for economic reality: (1) objective probabilities must exist; (2) subjective probabilities estimated as time averages must converge towards current objective probabilities; (3) current objective probabilities must be a good forecaster of the average of actual outcomes at future dates; and (4) economic agents must believe both past and future outcomes are the result of the same ergodic process.

If the government's objective is not to stabilize the economy but to remain in power, it may be in the government's interest to hide information and fool the public. Then any version of the REH would be wrong (Struthers, 1984, p. 1145; Maddock and Carter, 1982, p. 46).

It is claimed that the narrow version of RE is able to resolve fundamental disagreements among economists about the true theoretical model, such as disagreements between monetarist and Keynesian views of market clearing. Bausor, among others, points out that the fundamental nature of the narrow version of RE is grounded in equilibrium analysis:

> . . . claiming that the actual forecast errors are nonautoregressive and have mean zero effectively asserts that the underlying relationships controlling the economy are constant, known, and known to be constant. Consequently 'rationality' shrinks to the stochastic euphemism for perfect information. Finally, rational-expectations analysis is equilibrium analysis. The actual contracting, producing, and accumulating that people accomplish, as well as macroeconomic stabilisation policy, do not, on average, matter. Tethered to its preordained equilibrium, the model is trapped in logical time. It cannot emerge into the more general realm of non-equilibrium analysis (Bausor, 1983, p. 9).

In *The General Theory* Lord Keynes wrote that 'a theory cannot claim to be a *general* theory, unless it is applicable to the case where (or the range within which) money wages are fixed, just as much as to any other case'.[13] David Begg's solution (1982: book, pp. 68–9) to this dilemma is to relax the narrow version's information availability assumption – that is, to employ a form of generalized rational expectations – so that sufficient disaggregation will exist to allow different groups to have different information and form different expectations. No other solution seems viable since the concept of expectational equilibrium embedded in narrow RE analysis is by its very nature antithetical to differential information. A form of the narrow version

> ... seems to allude to a set of expectations that are somehow in 'equilibrium', even when equilibrium may not exist in the economy as a whole, and indeed may be both unachievable and undesirable. Yet, by permitting errors on the part of rational economic agents, it sets in motion a 'disequilibrium' process that itself provides for individuals to acquire information of a better grade, which in cost-benefit fashion they can utilize to revise their behavior. . . . However in highlighting gains and losses in the context of information gathering it does not address itself to the question of differential access to information. Rather, it dismisses this complication by saying that the fact that one individual has more 'superior' information than another can itself be viewed as relevant information to consider and respond to (Struthers, 1984, pp. 1138–9).

Other objections

One of the most common complaints against RE has been that the narrow version requires solving forward over all future time. It is argued that these computational feats cannot be accomplished by the majority of individuals whose expectations we wish to model. This criticism has been countered in two ways. First, it is not necessary for individuals themselves to perform the mental gymnastics implied by the evaluation of the forward-looking path. Government, academics and businesses publish information which is disseminated for a small fee. Second, one can simply bypass the problem by adopting the generalized form of RE. Individuals are then required to undertake the process themselves, but 'the presumption that individuals on average guess correctly must be considerably weakened' (Begg, 1982: book, p. 260) because rationality no longer equates market expectations with the true mathematical expectations conditional on all information.

A non-uniqueness problem exists if the saddlepoint property for stability is not met. Explosive behaviour, known in the literature as 'speculative bubbles', occurs most frequently when information is scarce. Burmeister (1980) argues that the practical use of the narrow versions of RE is severely limited because explosive behaviour appears to be the rule and not the exception. Robert Shiller (1978, p. 39), echoing Burmeister's results, draws the conclusion that 'even if a model does eventually converge on a rational expectations equilibrium, it may take such a long time to do so that, since the structure of the economy changes occasionally, the economy is never close to a rational expectations equilibrium'. The above-stated qualms with the narrow version have nonetheless been dispelled by some economists on the grounds that since we do not observe prices exploding off into infinity we need only consider the converging cases (Maddock and Carter, 1982, p. 45).

Some economists assert that the narrow versions of RE are inconsistent with uncertainty in historical time. These narrow forms deny historical time and uncertainty because they depend upon the concept of risk, which exists in a world of repetitive events in logical time (Forman, 1980; Bausor, 1983). Indeed many criticisms turn to a great extent on the uncertainty notion – a typically Austrian theme. *Ad hoc* models assumed that agents have too little uncertainty about the process which generates prices. The narrow versions of RE, however, incorporate uncertainty as randomness; without random factors there would be perfect foresight. Hence these have been dubbed 'stochastic perfect foresight models'. According to Struthers (1984, p. 1139), these models also underplay the role of uncertainty, but in a sense quite different from the logic of the *ad hoc* models and much closer to that of the classical perfect certainty models. Poole (1976, p. 504) characterizes the problem in the following passage:

> Rational-expectations theory might be regarded, in principle, as only slightly amending perfect-certainty models. One need only substitute the assumption of perfect knowledge of probability distributions for the assumption of perfect knowledge of outcomes. For the problems in which distributions are reasonably stable and in which the distributions can be estimated, stochastic models quite clearly have been productive.

But Poole reminds the reader that business cycle theory is not analogous to gambling behaviour. There are no rules of the game; the environment and knowledge of it are constantly in flux. He remains uneasy, not so much because of the substitution of stochastic models for certainty models, but because the literature offers little 'guidance for predicting the speed with which economic agents learn of the changed odds' (Poole, 1976, pp. 504–505).

Arrow suggests that the emphasis on future time is too extreme, as was adaptive expectation's emphasis on past time. He praises the weight given to stocks and expectations as a corrective balance to the preoccupation with flows which has marked post-Keynesian thinking. But he cautions that the RE new classical models also embody assumptions which are too drastic:

> Clearly, we do not expect people to be consistently wrong in their judgements, at least as based on data available to them. I recognize also that the influence of the future on the present is powerful and that many actions of a short run nature can be expected to have little effect when they can be so easily offset when anticipated. But an appropriate development of macroeconomic theory and its reconciliation with microeconomic foundations demands more complete attention to the information bases of anticipations and how they differ from individual to individual in a dispersed economy.[14]

Subjectivists deny the existence of a true or objective probability distribution apart from the beliefs of agents. They see probability beliefs as bets an individual would be willing to make about the occurrence of events and argue that, if choices among bets satisfy certain axioms, a consistent subjective probability measure can be derived for the individual. Individual probability beliefs need not coincide with each other or with an objective probability distribution (Sheffrin, 1983: book, p. 12). Lucas has defended the narrow version of RE by stating that the subjectivist or Bayesian approach does not help in understanding behaviour and has no empirical content. Swamy, Barth and Tinsley (1982) argue, however, that the conventional formulations of the REH violate the axiomatic basis of statistical theory by confusing objective and subjective concepts of probability. They maintain that testing the rationality of subjective expectations by comparison with observable frequencies is logically impossible. (It is no wonder, then, that Muth encloses 'objective' in quotation marks when defining RE in his famous 1961 paper.) Swamy, Barth and Tinsley discuss the fact that there are at least three different definitions of objective probability currently in use. They conclude that the consistent formulation of narrow RE is too restrictive to be of practical benefit.

The narrow version of RE must be linear or it loses its certainty equivalence property. Individuals, however, may not only care about the mean of future random variables, but also about other measures of their statistical distributions such as variances. Nevertheless, these extensions and the subsequent violation of the certainty equivalence property would make manipulation of the resulting nonlinear models quite difficult (Begg, 1982: book, p. 263).

Wible (1982–83) argues that the theory is tautological; in other words, the theoretical and policy-making principles restate the consequences of rationality and of efficient competitive markets which theorists have already employed to explain the narrow versions.

The concept of equilibrium becomes complicated. First, the traditional notion of equilibrium is expanded. Not only must markets clear, but there must be no systematic falsification of 'rationally' formed expectations.[15]

Oxley shows how defining supply and demand curves becomes quite messy. Traditional curves represent the mean value of agents' actions and are denoted by solid lines; broken lines depict variance around the mean. Points lying off the demand and supply curves and within the interval for the mean represent equilibria due to random disturbances without market clearing. Oxley (1983, p. 186) explains that an equilibrium in a narrow RE expectations framework can fail anywhere between WXYZ.

A statistical identification problem exists: is it possible, in principle, to retrieve separate estimates of all the relevant theoretical parameters of the

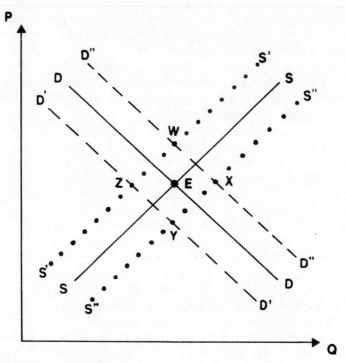

Equilibrium in a RE model

model from the data? Expectations based on an incorrect view of the model will affect behaviour and therefore also the data to be used in empirical work which seeks to quantify the model (Begg, 1982: book, pp. 65–7).

Another related problem is the distinction between the formation of expectations and their efficient use. Efficient use of irrational expectations ordinarily cannot be distinguished from inefficient use of rational expectations (Poole, 1976, p. 468).

A transition problem also exists because simply knowing the model does not necessarily make people behave rationally in a Muth or narrow RE sense. If economic agents do settle on a RE solution in the future, they may not act rationally today (Shiller, 1978, pp. 37–8).

Related to this is the fact that Muth and others assume that the relevant model is the correct model in describing objective reality. Colander and Guthrie (1980–81) point out that if this were not the case, then agents would discard an incorrect model in favour of another which may or may not be correct. This implies that there must be a 'rational' method of alternative model selection, thus doubling the level of 'rationality'. Since the same applies to discarding incorrect models, 'every REH model is of an infinite order of rationality' (Colander and Guthrie, 1980–81, p. 222). Stephen DeCanio cautions:

> Unless all agents at all times form rational expectations, the 'structure' deter-
> mining the realizations of the forecast variable will evolve over time as the
> forecasting sophistication of the agents changes. This point is similar to Lucas'
> (1976) observation that shifts in policy will change the 'structural' parameters
> of the economic system depending on how agents react to the policies (DeCa-
> nio, 1979, p. 55).

In addition, to satisfy the narrow version of RE, agents must have identical expectations (Haberler, 1980(b)) which must be based upon the same model. Even if agents totally comprehend the economic structure as it currently exists, the economy is subject to occasional and unpredictable changes which could 'render the once well-understood historical relationships obsolete' (Berkman, 1980, p. 26).

Yet no one would argue with the fact that economists themselves do not know, or agree on, what the correct model is:

> We cannot test the hypothesis until we find the right model and the rational
> formation of expectations is a part of the model. Since there is little consensus
> about the correctness of most estimated models, clearly one could prolong the
> debate about whether the hypothesis has been rejected or not almost indefi-
> nitely, as it could always be the model which is at fault (Mayes, 1981, p. 57).

Frydman *et al.* (1982) point out that whether or not it is a unique and relevant theory, the narrow version remains a clear and viable concept. However, if there are multiple relevant economic theories and if no one knows which theory the agent believes, then the narrow version remains undefined. The authors analyse this problem within a prisoner's dilemma framework. When there are multiple relevant theories, the behaviour of the decision-maker must also be predicted:

> In such situations, a rational expectation about the level of such a variable
> becomes a prediction of the behavior of the decision maker who controls its
> value. The problem is that if the decision maker's payoffs depend upon whether
> its behavior is anticipated or not, then the decision maker will be forced to enter
> into a series of higher order expectations in his effort to try to second-guess
> those agents who are forming rational expectations over his behavior. The
> knowledge that others are trying to predict a decision maker's behavior in a
> systematic (i.e., rational) way may force the decision maker to behave non-

systematically and hence eliminate any hope of forming a rational expectation about his behavior (Frydman *et al.*, 1982, p. 319).

Although we have by no means exhausted the many published criticisms and qualifications of the narrow version of the REH, this sample clearly shows how problematic the narrow version is.

4   The question of stabilization polic

The most controversial application of RE has been to stabilization policy. 'It is instructive', writes Shaw (1987, p. 187), 'that Muth has remained remarkably aloof from the macroeconomic controversies generated by the concept which he introduced into economic science.' The policy neutrality conclusions have been produced solely by new classical models, which were able to merge the narrow version of the REH with the natural rate hypothesis (NRH).

The first paper in macroeconomics to derive a 'Phillips curve'[16] with all agents behaving optimally and with expectations formed rationally in the narrow sense was Lucas' 'Expectations and the Neutrality of Money', published in 1972. This paper and subsequent works by Sargent, Wallace and Barro form the foundations of new classical equilibrium macro-economics.[17] Most of the subsequent controversy has centred around two policy propositions drawn from their works; namely, (1) that the antici-pated or systematic component of nominal aggregate demand affects only the price level and not the real variables, which may be influenced solely by unexpected components; and (2) that the unexpected component of demand is stochastic and hence unforeseen by authorities as well as by the public. Thus the authorities have no power to influence real variables by demand management policies.

New classical theoretical results build upon the works of Friedman and Phelps in which the formation and effects of inflationary expectations were developed.[18] Since these are natural rate models, the first requirement is to understand the NRH.

The Phillips curve and the natural rate hypothesis
The Phillips curve is attributed to A. W. Phillips, who in 1958 postulated a negative relationship between inflation (π) and unemployment (U). The Phillips curve is represented in its familiar graphical form below.

The behavioural assumptions justifying this relationship can be summed up as follows. When U is relatively low, firms find it hard to attract workers and thus tend to bid up wages. In the opposite situation, where many workers are available, the pressure on wages ceases. The Phillips curve relationship could be exploited by policy-makers: by toler-ating higher inflation, for instance, unemployment could be reduced. The

23

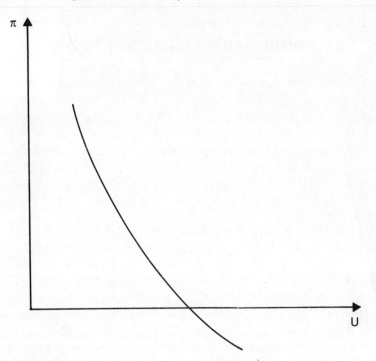

The Phillips curve

Phillips curve became an integral part of the Keynesian orthodoxy of the 1960s.

Friedman was the first to reject the tradeoff implied by the Phillips curve. In his 1967 presidential address before the American Economic Association, Friedman coined the term 'natural rate of employment' and defined it as follows:

> the level (of employment) that would be ground out by the Walrasian system of general equilibrium equations provided there is embedded in them the actual structural characteristics of the labor and commodity markets, including market imperfections, stochastic variability in demands and supplies, the cost of gathering information about job vacancies and labor availabilities, the costs of mobility, and so on.[19]

He proceeded to outline the acceleration corollary:

> There is always a temporary trade-off between inflation and unemployment; there is no permanent trade-off. The temporary trade-off comes not from

inflation per se, but from unanticipated inflation, which generally means a rising rate of inflation.[20]

In other words, when inflation is fully anticipated and markets clear, unemployment is equal to its natural rate. Friedman and Phelps emphasize that unanticipated inflation can have real effects because workers err in the short run when a general price rise affecting both wages and prices occurs; they mistake it for a specific price rise in the market for their own labour services. Hence, these 'natural rate theories rely on an asymmetry in sources of price information; the worker knows his offer before he knows the price level, and the firm knows the price of the labor it hires' (Shiller, 1978, p. 8).

This means that the use of monetary expansion to reduce unemployment below the natural rate fails. Only if actual monetary expansion exceeds the expected rate can employment be increased temporarily. If the government wants to reduce unemployment by using expansionary policy, inflation will accelerate and the short-run Phillips curve will shift upwards as shown in the diagram below. In the long run the Phillips curve is vertical.

The algebraic formulation of the expectations-augmented Phillips curve is given below:

$$\pi = \pi^e + \alpha(U - U_n), (\alpha > 0)$$

where π is the actual inflation rate, π^e is the expected inflation rate, U is the actual unemployment rate and U_n is the natural unemployment rate. Because attempts to reduce unemployment result in accelerating inflation, the monetary authority should follow a consistent monetary growth rule rather than an activist stabilization policy. In sum, the basic characteristics of the Friedman NRH are as follows:

1. Being ground out by a Walrasian system, it corresponds to the amount of unemployment that occurs when the labour market displays neither excess supply nor demand and when output is at full-employment level. Thus it is not compatible with disequilibrium analysis.[21]
2. The corresponding Phillips curve is vertical; there is no permanent or long-run tradeoff between inflation and unemployment.
3. 'Fooling' workers or other misperceptions can cause deviations from natural levels of output and employment – a Phillips curve – in the short run.
4. Policy is efficacious only in the short run because in the long run people cannot be fooled.

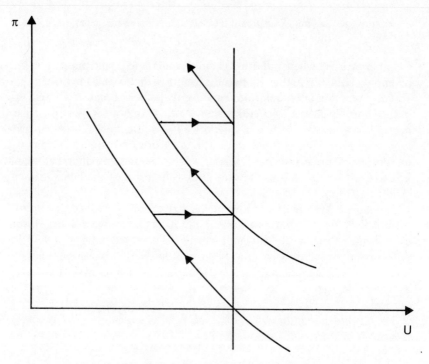

The expectations-augmented Phillips curve

The NRH as developed by Phelps was not embedded in a particular market-clearing model. Furthermore, the various natural rate models depend on a variety of *ad hoc* assumptions to explain short-run deviations of output from the natural rate. Most models depend on the asymmetry of information between suppliers and demanders with respect to (1) expectation formation, (2) price-decision variables, and (3) access to information.[22]

To be sure, the NRH is as ambiguous a concept as rational expectations. The literature abounds with allusions to strong, weak, extreme or dogmatic versions. Whether due to disagreement, sloppiness or ideological preferences within the discipline, the concept has been defined by one, some or all of the four components of Friedman's NRH. More general definitions have extended the NRH to the non-market-clearing world and have accepted reasons other than fooling workers to explain deviations in output and employment from natural levels. In a recent article, for instance, Herschel Grossman has described the NRH as a 'robust proposition' and asserted that given the microeconomic structure of the economy, the behavior of private economic agents – businessmen, workers, and consumers – that is based on correct expectations about the rate of inflation generates unique levels of aggregate output, employment, and unemployment, denoted for obscure historical reasons as 'natural' levels (H. Grossman, 1980, p. 7).

The new classical Phillips curve and the policy neutrality proposition

The narrow version of RE combined with the NRH as originally advanced by Lucas (1981(a) and 1972) and Sargent (1973 (a and b)) defines expected inflation as 'the optimally forecasted rate of inflation based on all information available' (Shiller, 1978, p. 9). Since prices are forecast optimally, economic agents should not be systematically fooled as is assumed by the Friedman NRH. When agents form expectations rationally, anticipated actions of the monetary authority will be incorporated into the agents' expectations of inflation: people will not be fooled by systematic policy even in the short run. Thus only unanticipated changes in the money supply can make the actual inflation rate diverge from the expected rate.

Most models which incorporate the new classical joint combination of the REH-NRH share several characteristic features. First, the idea that levels of income and prices are determined by the intersection of aggregate supply and demand where the former is taken to be vertical; in this way output cannot deviate from the natural level as a result of a change in the level of demand. Second, optimal forecast of the inflation rate is guaranteed because individuals behave as if they know what the objective joint probability distribution is for inflation and all other economic variables (Shiller, 1978, p. 9).

The earliest version (see Lucas, 1972; Barro, 1981(a)) of the Friedman NRH merged with the narrow version of the REH – the new classical Phillips curve – resulting in a redefinition of the NRH as an aggregate supply function of the form:

$$y_t = y_n + \alpha(p_t - E_t(p_{t+1} / I_t)) + u_t^s, \alpha > 0$$

where y_t is the natural log of real output at time t; p_t is the natural log of the price level at time t; y_n is the natural log of the natural rate of ouput, and u_t^s is a serially uncorrelated random supply disturbance term with mean zero. This version of the NRH is variously called the Lucas supply function, the Lucas-Sargent aggregate supply function or, following Buiter, 'the Friedman-Lucas-instantaneous-natural rate or only-wage-and-price-surprises matter' supply function (Buiter, 1980, p. 34). From this equation we can see that output at time t deviates from its natural level by an amount proportional to the last period's prediction error and the supply disturbance. In this version the response of supply ($y_t - y_n$) to prices depends on the intertemporal substitutability of leisure.

This supply function is derived from a two-period consumer decision model in which consumers must choose between current and future consumption of goods and leisure. The aggregate supply curve is more often formulated in the version below (Sargent and Wallace, 1975 and Sargent, 1973 (a and b) and 1976), where the dating of expectations has been altered to

$$y_t = y_n + \alpha(p_t - E_{t-1}(p_t / I_{t-1})) + u_t^s, \alpha > 0.$$

A 'Phillips curve' is generated via informational error: suppliers of labour and goods mistake aggregate price changes as relative changes because they receive information about prices of their own goods before that about the aggregate price level. Robert Gordon (1981, p. 505) claims that the 'Lucas supply function' should be renamed the 'Friedman supply function' because it naturally builds on Friedman's AER address and on Phelps' island parable. It must be remembered, however, that Phelps' agents are not exposed to aggregate phenomena (they exist on isolated islands), whereas Lucas' agents are aware of aggregate phenomena but cannot always distinguish aggregate changes from local shocks. The Lucas supply curve has several notable characteristics: the relationship is linear, the forecasts are optimal, and deviations of employment and output from their natural levels are due to forecast errors. If no forecast errors occur, output and unemployment remain at their normal levels.

Another version of the new classical Phillips curve and a more general form of the above expression is

$$u_t = u_n - \beta(p_t - E_{t-1}(p_t/I_{t-1})) + \epsilon_t^s, \beta > 0,$$

where u_t is the actual level of unemployment, u_n is the natural rate of unemployment, and ϵ_t^s is the random supply disturbance with mean 0 and no serial correlation. If there were a strictly linear relationship between y_t and u_t, both expressions would be equivalent (Shiller, 1978, p. 9). Variations of this general form can be found in the works of Lucas, Sargent and Wallace, McCallum, Fischer, and Taylor.

In some models (e.g. Lucas, 1973) the coefficients alpha and beta are not constant but rather inversely related to the variance of the price level. The significance of the variance hypothesis is that the larger the variance of monetary and fiscal behaviour, the smaller the effects of given unpredictable and unperceivable monetary and fiscal actions on aggregate output and employment (H. Grossman, 1980, p. 12).

The information availability assumption plays a crucial role in establishing classical conclusions in a model incorporating one of the many variations of the Lucas supply function. The difference between the current price level and the economic agent's previous period expectation of the current price level, $p_t - E_{t-1}(p_t / I_{t-1})$, determines the deviation of output from its natural level. According to the deviation defined by the narrow version of the REH,

$$p_t = E_{t-1}(p_t / I_{t-1}) + \epsilon_t.$$

Thus, the public's expectations of p_t, conditional on information available at time $t - 1$, differ from p_t itself only by an error which is pure white noise, ϵ_t. To find the conditional expectation, agents must solve the model using its own mathematical expectation in the equation; hence agents must know not only the specification of the other equations in the model but also the values of their coefficients (B. Friedman, 1979, p. 27).

The neutrality of monetary policy follows naturally from the specific rendering of the new classical Phillips curve. Movements of the money stock may affect output by influencing forecast errors. Agents have sufficient information to assess the model's impact on the price of any given value of the money stock. Agents then form their conditional expectations accordingly; the prediction error is independent of, or orthogonal to, the money stock, as it is of all other conditioning variables. In other words, 'the available information always includes sufficient knowledge to generate expectations which are orthogonal to all underlying conditioning variables' (B. Friedman, 1979, p. 38). As a result, the expected values of u_t and of y_t will equal y_n despite the policy rule followed because the stochastic behaviour of the government has been taken into account in the formation of conditional expectations. This result is at the core of the new classical version of the NRH and justifies the conclusion that government policy is essentially impotent.[23]

It is most unfortunate that these results were at first assumed to constitute *every* fundamental rational expectations model, and that some economists still talk about the RE school when they mean new classical economics. The results, however, reflect the assumptions embedded within the new classical models. That is, the new classical conclusions drawn from the model are not catholic invariance results; they do not derive from the rational expectations hypothesis *per se*, but from a set of highly restrictive assumptions built into the model. Lee (1984, p. 154) sums up the message of these new classical models: 'The old view that government can manage the economy by fooling people is thus neatly replaced by the idea that people can fool – and foil – government policymakers'. As Sir Denis Robertson once remarked: 'highbrow opinion is like a hunted hare;

if you stand in the same place, or nearly the same place, it can be relied upon to come round to you in a circle'.[24]

Amendment for the persistence problem

Lucas explained business cycles using models in which labour markets clear and thus contain no notion of involuntary unemployment. The orthogonality property of conditional expectations requires errors to be uncorrelated over time. Levels of output are also uncorrelated, the only source of deviation from full employment being random forecast errors (Sheffrin, book: 1983, p. 55). Hence, if output is greater than full employment in one period, forecasts of the next period's output should nonetheless be at full-employment level. The empirical evidence, however, rejects this implication: booms and recessions generally continue to the next period, while movements of output, employment and unemployment also persist. The early new classical model failed to explain such persistent, serially correlated business cycle movements and thus had to be amended.

First Lucas introduced a lagged dependent variable to the Lucas supply curve, with the justification that not all of the deviation could be accounted for in the expectation term (Lucas, 1972). Later he postulated that because agents do not realize that they have made forecast errors until several periods later, these errors can be correlated. (The reasoning behind this behavioural assumption is rather abstract and utilizes the island parable in what has become known as the 'signal extraction' problem: when information is not perfect, a producer must distinguish between permanent and temporary, real and nominal, components of his selling price.)

Lucas makes it clear that a theory of the persistent business cycle cannot be founded on the narrow version of RE (Lucas, 1981(d), pp. 179–80 and 1113–14). According to Poole, however, the introduction of information lags can produce persistence, but the device seems to bring us back to adaptive expectations (Poole, 1976, p. 483). Minford and Peel (1982) warn the reader that the disequilibrium foundation of the conventional Phillips curve is not sustained in the new classical models which are based on equilibrium microfoundations. 'Great care therefore must be taken not to interpret RE Phillips curves in the Phillips-Lipsey-Phelps tradition' (Minford and Peel, 1982, p. 451).

Explosion of the policy neutrality myth

The policy neutrality proposition has its roots in the following new classical assumptions (Shiller, 1983, p. 46):

1. the debt neutrality theorem – that future tax payments are fully discounted by the public;
2. the hypothesis of flexible prices and of output deviations due to current price deviations from expected prices (i.e., the particular specification of the Lucas aggregate supply function); and
3. the information structure built into the model.

In short, by using a more general model – one which disregards the above assumptions or incorporates multiple commodities, multiperiod wage contracts, dating of expectations, etc. – the invariance result vanishes.

Monetary policy's efficacy was rejuvenated by Fischer (1977) and Phelps and Taylor (1977). They show that rigidities in prices due to wage or price contracts allow monetary policy to be effective in stabilizing the variance of output and inflation. Actual output differs from the natural rate not because of price or forecast error – which would indicate a violation of the Friedman NRH – but because an information-action hiatus exists whose potential was agreed upon in advance by workers and employers and crystallized and legalized in contract form. More specifically, at any point in time public and private agents have the same information set so that misperceptions do not occur; because the private agent is contractually bound by the past, only the public agent is free to respond to new information. Since private agents may not adequately respond to a fully anticipated change in public sector policy to undo all of its real effects, deviations in output and employment may occur. As Fischer explains,

> The effectiveness of monetary policy does not require anyone to be fooled. In the model of Section III, with two-period contracts, monetary policy is fully anticipated but because it is based on information which becomes available after the labor contract is made, it can affect output. If the monetary authority wants to stabilize output, it can do so. . . (Fischer, 1977, p. 203).

Sargent and Wallace (1975) also establish a role for monetary policy should the information sets of monetary authorities and private agents differ. It has been argued that the assumed information structure does not reflect the institutional structure of the US economy. But Snower disagrees. He suspects that the monetary authority may simply have a greater incentive to gain an informational advantage:

> After all, unsystematic variations in the money supply may be the outcome of policy surprises engineered by the monetary authority. Whenever the monetary authority does so, it automatically has an information advantage concerning the surprise, and thereby systematic monetary policy becomes potent (Snower, 1984, p. 180).

Minford and Peel (1981) went a step further, arguing that even in the absence of the two conditions mentioned above, there is still scope for stabilization policy. They classify various supply specifications used to capture the NRH and, after modifying the hypothesis in small ways, comment:

> These conclusions do not depend on assuming multi-period contracts. It appears that the minimum conditions required for stabilization of output to be feasible are that first, the supply hypothesis is not of the Sargent/Wallace form. ... Secondly, that there are inflation effects in the IS schedule and, thirdly, that there are lags in the model due to either persistence effects or moving average error processes (Minford and Peel, 1981, p. 49).

Adrian Pagan and Alan Preston confirm that the stabilization outcome depends upon the particular macro model in which the REH and NRH are embedded. Developing a more general model that incorporates narrow RE with the NRH as a particular case, they show that 'impact controllability' (a mathematical formulation of stabilization effectiveness) depends upon a rank condition, which in turn depends upon the specification of the model. The necessary and sufficient condition for the existence of policy efficacy according to them is 'the onto mapping from instrument to target space'. Moreover, 'the mere presence of rational expectations in a model will [not] mean the loss of the onto property and hence controllability'.[25]

Many authors alter the information structure. B. Friedman (1979) and Cyert and DeGroot (1974) specify learning functions. Feige and Pearce (1976, p. 499) claim that their 'economically rational' expectations are 'a middle ground between "autoregressive" expectation formation and "rational" expectation formation'. Weiss (1980) constructs a model in which some agents have access to investment information before others. He again shows that the presence of asymmetric information allows stabilization policy to be effective. Peter Howitt (1981) criticizes the policy neutrality results because they ignore both the costs of gathering information and any uncertainty about the structure of the economic system; he builds models incorporating these elements and finds that policy may be effective. Duck (1983) uses a new classical model but assumes that the money supply process is uncertain in being subject to abrupt, unpredictable shifts; forecast errors which exhibit persistence therefore occur.

Other features of the new classical models have also been altered. Blinder and Fischer (1981) generate business cycles through the gradual adjustment of inventory stocks. They allow random disturbances to affect the stock of inventories so that a price surprise which induces firms to sell out their inventories will lead to persistent movements of output. David

Begg (1980) develops a model in which a multiplicity of steady state paths exist so that the perfect foresight path[26] depends on the chosen rate of monetary growth. Money will not then be superneutral.[27] Snower (1984) argues that even if the NRH is joined with the narrow version of the REH, systematic monetary policy may be efficacious if the macroeconomic model is nonlinear. Snower does not amend the REH version of the NRH used in the new classical models. Shiller (1978) also shows that the assumption of linearity determines the policy conclusion.

Buiter (1980) suggests that optimal allocation decisions of private actors will be affected by changes in prices, but not just because agents are fooled. The neutrality of money is violated because portfolio readjustments are necessary when inflation changes the real rate of return on financial assets which have a zero nominal return. Models incorporating a narrow version of RE assume that the only reason for holding money is the transactions motive. If prices rise, the desire to hold money falls, changing people's allocation decisions and perhaps the rate of capital formation or number of hours worked. Buiter implicitly rejects Barro's debt neutrality theorem[28] which he believes constitutes nothing more than a 'theoretical curiosum' (Buiter, 1980, p. 40). He concludes that the labour market decision is not independent of price increases allowing for employment and output deviations because changes in the money stock influence such factors as agents' preferred hours of work and portfolio holdings.

As a final note, if the 'people-prefer-to-avoid-the-consequences-of-policy' notion is turned on its head then, as Maddock and Carter (1982, p. 48) explain, 'If businessmen understand the economic implications of expansionary government policy, they can expand their output in anticipation of those effects rather than waiting for the rise in demand to be obvious in the market. In that case, far from being impotent, rational expectations may make policy *more* effective.'

Further problems with new classical analysis: conceptual difficulties and limitations

It is often assumed that both unanticipated and anticipated policy can be clearly delineated, as for instance in Barro and Rush's work, 'Unanticipated Money and Economic Activity' (1980). Haberler (1980(b)) contends that the distinction between the two is rather fuzzy, as most government actions do not fall into neat categories which would allow systematic and unsystematic shocks to be separated. Fellner (1980) stresses that the policy inefficacy result rests on the assumption that the monetary authorities behave according to a system which can and will be understood by the public. McCallum replied to both of these critiques in a 1980 paper in the following way: 'For the issues at hand, it seems best to assume away (perhaps unrealistically) such inefficiencies' (McCallum, 1980(a), p. 725).

The randomness described in RE models may not be random at all, but may be a source of fluctuations generated by beliefs – that is, self-fulfilling prophecies. Given a well-behaved economy and a RE equilibrium, expectations themselves may create fluctuations in the level of economic activity. Costas Azariadis (1981) estimated one-third to one-half of all equilibria may be generated by self-fulfilling prophecies. If so, business cycles set in motion by arbitrary shifts influence price changes because they are expected (and not unexpected as in new classical RE models). Cass and Shell (1983) and Haberler (1980(b)) also echo themes of psychology-of-the-market-derived business cycles.[29]

The narrow version of RE works by means of price expectations, but these affect only some of the current markets. The market for perishable goods – including labour – is more sensitive to current prices than to price expectations. The demand for perishables is controlled by the wage factor and remains relatively unchanged with respect to expected price changes.[30]

New classical theory does not provide a foundation for the short-run Phillips curve. Cherry (1981) indicates that the models' assumptions are *ad hoc*. Minford and Peel (1983: book), on the other hand, point out that the Phillips (-Lipsey-Phelps) curve relationship undergoes conceptual transformation when joined with the new classical version of the NRH-REH. The Phillips (-Lipsey-Phelps) curve results from the dynamic adjustment process of the labour market in disequilibrium. Disequilibrium in turn occurs as workers search for the best wage bargain obtainable. The Lucas-Sargent-Wallace 'Phillips curve', on the other hand, is antithetical to the Phillips disequilibrium foundation. Temporary disequilibrium occurs only if expectations are wrong. As soon as error is discovered (and contracts renegotiated), equilibrium is re-established. Wages then clear the labour markets on the basis of expectations.

Even the Lucas critique has come under fire. In two papers (1972 and 1976) Lucas developed the thesis that standard macroeconomic modelling is faulty because the parameters of models are invariant with respect to changes in policy. The consequence is that simulations from these macro-economic models are not reliable unless policy is constant. As policy changes, economic agents will forecast the effects of that new policy and modify their behaviour accordingly. Effective modelling should take into consideration changing expectations. Lucas suggests that econometric techniques should incorporate the narrow REH to correct the problem. But the Lucas critique is not beyond reproach because it does not incorporate a learning process of agents. If learning is significant, especially following major policy changes, the techniques would not be valid for the short run. His critique also neglects the fact that other factors may shift the model parameters.

Begg (1980, p. 160) highlights the problem of the ambiguity of the NRH in non-market-clearing models, which can be defined in two different ways.

> [W]e might mean the level of output or unemployment which occurs if expectations formed in the previous period are indeed fulfilled, or the level of output or employment which corresponds to Walrasian market clearing in all markets. Only in the market-clearing world in which Friedman coined the term do the two definitions reduce to the same thing.

Finally, there are deep-seated semantic difficulties involved with both the REH and NRH concepts which are most unfortunate. 'Rational' implies that any other type of expectations' formation is irrational and hence wrong. The same applies to the word 'natural' of the NRH. Clear terminology and classifications are necessary to understand and communicate effectively. Although the terms 'rational' and 'natural' will certainly appeal to the neoclassical economist, such constructions are often interpreted as somehow more real than other characteristics of the phenomena, thus inviting confusion. It is not by chance that A.A. Walters (1971, p. 273) writes: 'I also prefer the label consistent to rational; that the expectation is consistent with a particular theory may be reasonably obvious – but rationality is another matter'. And Machlup (1983, p. 174) argues:

> I am using the term 'rational' expectations under protest, since rational and correct are quite different things. Economists who had read *Max Weber* – and at one time every educated economist was supposed to have done so – have agreed that rationality meant consistency with one's preconceptions and prejudgements, right or wrong. . . . *John Muth* may be charged with an infraction of terminological discipline when he misused the term 'rational' to denote 'correct' expectations (or expectations in conformance with those of some economic theorists of the neoclassical school).

Moreover, the use of 'expectations' is technically incorrect since 'expect' and 'anticipate' are not synonymous. To anticipate something is to expect it and to react accordingly. With regard to the REH, 'anticipations' would be a more accurate term because the hypothesis assumes that the anticipation of some future change in economic variables will have an immediate effect on the economy.[31]

5 Is the rational expectations controversy merely a debate about market-clearing and non-market-clearing models?

In 1976 Robert A. Gordon described RE as a theory which 'proceeds with impeccable logic from unrealistic assumptions to conclusions that contradict the historical record'.[32] In 1982 McCallum realized that 'major differences continue to exist' between those who do and do not support the narrow version of the REH, but 'the terms of disagreement are no longer about the hypothesis of rational expectations – some version of the latter is utilized in almost all current research – but about the nature of the economy within which agents operate and form expectations'.[33]

Certainly it has been argued that labour markets do not function efficiently[34] and hence that equilibrium analysis does not adequately capture the essence of the subject matter. Colander and Guthrie (1980–81) argue that '. . . Muth turned disequilibrium into equilibrium', while Arrow explains further that

> . . . the choice between these viewpoints is deeply related to the existence of involuntary unemployment. The view that only real magnitudes matter can be defended only if it is assumed that the labor market (and all other markets) always clear – that is, that all unemployment is essentially voluntary. In this theory, individuals may be unemployed because of errors of judgement – they believe that higher wages can be found by search or waiting. But, it is held, at each moment there is a going wage, and any worker who wishes to work at that wage can do so. The view that only real magnitudes matter, even over the short periods of the business cycle, can be defended on this extreme view of smoothly working labor markets. If the contrary view is held, that actual unemployment is to a considerable extent involuntary, then monetary magnitudes retain some of their traditional importance for the analysis of and policy toward short-term economic fluctuations.[35]

Taylor provides a useful framework from which to understand the schism in stabilization policy.[36] Theories may be considered as either 'information-based' or 'contract-based'. Information-based theories explain disturbances as the result of two types of uncertainties about the economy: (a) uncertainty about whether a change is local or economy-wide, or (b) uncertainty about whether a change is temporary or permanent. By assuming that prices adjust instantaneously to clear markets, these theories lay claim to a compatibility with microeconomic foundations. Contract-based theories, on the other hand, postulate temporary rigidities in wages and prices with an emphasis on (a) relative price shifts due to asymmetrical rigidities, and (b) the general persistence of all prices due to non-synchronous price or wage setting relative to a prevailing trend in prices and wages. Markets clear in the sense that supply equals demand in the short run; in the long run prices adjust to clear markets. Contract-based theories are said to more closely approximate actual practice regarding goods and labour markets. It should be clear that information-based theories are compatible with contracts only in the highly restrictive sense when wages and prices are not set beyond a market-clearing period. Indeed McCallum makes the point that wage and price stickiness may be assumed without abandoning equilibrium analysis.[37]

Some economists, including those in the new classical school, are suspicious of contract theory because its theoretical structure hangs on 'an as yet absent theory of the stickiness of wages and prices'.[38] Contract theory lacks microfoundations; it is *ad hoc*. Worse, if contracts are really responsible for fluctuations in output and employment, why are they written? Despite the contentions of Barro and others that contract theory has no sound theoretical basis, no consensus exists on the issue. Buiter, citing recent work on equilibrium in markets with imperfect and costly information, concludes that

> socially inefficient quantity constrained (rationing) equilibria with sticky prices can be generated by privately rational optimizing behavior. Hence non-market-clearing models aren't *ad hoc* in the sense of depicting situations in which not all feasible trades that are to the perceived mutual advantage of the exchanging parties have been exhausted (Buiter, 1980, p. 41).

Nonetheless Sanford Grossman maintains that, if an economy is characterized by traders having differential information, the new classical models differ radically from Walrasian models. He raises the point that prices function as signals only in stochastic economies. In nonstochastic economies agents are constrained by prices, but nonetheless in a way which will very often lead to collective rationality (S. Grossman, 1981, p. 544) so that the REH serves as a 'sufficient statistic for all of the economy's information' (p. 555). It should be noted, however, that Grossman assumes a complete set of future markets in order to obtain these results and admits that there is little empirical evidence to support the theoretical conclusions.

In all fairness, both the informational assumptions of equilibrium theorists as well as the postulation of contracts are *ad hoc* in nature. Discussing this issue in detail, Lowenberg (1982) remarks that 'information gaps play the same role in the new classical macrorational expectations models as the failure of prices to clear markets in Keynesian models, and are equally arbitrary'.

RE equilibrium models create business cycles by incorporating asymmetries in information: agents cannot distinguish between aggregate and market disturbances or between real and nominal shocks. In a few models, the monetary authority has an informational advantage. In non-Walrasian, or Keynesian, models price rigidity causes business cycles. Price rigidity is explained by oligopolistic pricing practices, transactions or information costs (which make it too costly for wages and prices to adjust instantaneously), multi-period contracts, or heterogeneity of goods and factors. As Oxley emphasizes in the passage below, the issue remains moot:

> What becomes more and more obvious is that differences between economists' views are not in relation to R.E. but *feelings* about whether markets clear. I emphasize 'feelings' because as yet no clear evidence has been presented one way or the other (Oxley, 1983, p. 184).

An overview of these fundamental differences in viewing the market and its workings is provided below. This is a simplified version adapted from Blinder's very readable and amusing (1987) article, 'Keynes, Lucas, and Scientific Progress'.

Differences between Keynesian and new classical economics (NCE): an overview
1. Are expectations rational?
    NCE: Yes, in the narrow sense.
    Keynesian: Yes, in the generalized sense.
2. Is there involuntary unemployment?
    NCE: No, the unemployed are searching for jobs or prefer to be unemployed (i.e., unemployment is treated as leisure).
    Keynesian: Certainly. When unemployment rises, statistics reveal that it is layoffs, not quits, which have risen.
3. Do wage movements clear the labour market quickly?
    NCE: Yes.
    Keynesian: No. The labour market is not an efficient market.
4. Is the natural rate of employment a useful concept?
    NCE: Yes.
    Keynesian: Yes in the long run, but the Phillips curve relationship holds in the short run.
5. Is there a reliable Phillips curve relationship?
    NCE: No, that was the Keynesian demise.

Keynesian: Yes, but in the 1970s it needed to be modified for supply shocks; despite problems, it is still one of the best-behaved empirical relationships in the history of macroeconomics.

6. Do changes in the money supply have real effects?
   NCE: Yes, when unanticipated.
   Keynesian: Yes.
7. Does social welfare rise when business cycles are limited?
   NCE: Stabilization policies are counterproductive. Lucas explains (in Lee, 1984, p. 147): 'Since nobody understands deeply how the economy responds, it's best not to try anything fancy'.
   Keynesian: Yes, that is one goal of the US Employment Act of 1946, which aims at economic stability and growth.
8. Should macroeconomics be based on firm microeconomic foundations?
   NCE: Yes, definitely.
   Keynesian: No. Keynes didn't think so.

In addition, McMahon (1984(b)) has developed a schema for quickly surveying the significance of expectations in market-clearing (MC) and non-market-clearing (NMC) models. McMahon maintains that there are three states of expectations which have been embedded in market-clearing and non-market-clearing models. His framework has been transformed into the table below:

1. All economic agents have the same expectations and they are correct.
   MC economics: Full-information economics.
   NMC economics: Neo-Keynesian disequilibrium models.
2. All agents have the same expectations, but they are incorrect.
   MC economics: New classical macroeconomics of Lucas.
   NMC economics: Neoclassical synthesis (Klein, Patinkin)
3. Expectations are different and some are wrong
   MC economics: Models of Wicksell, Friedman and of Keynes' *Treatise*.
   NMC economics: Keynes' *General Theory*.

In a spirit of cooperation, macroeconomists have come much closer in the 1980s. Robert Gordon (1981, pp. 494ff.) has suggested that the MC-NMC dispute be resolved by merging the more convincing elements of both views. Indeed some version of the REH has been accepted by both sides. Leijonhufvud (1983(b), p. 200) has reached the surprising conclusion that a 'more detailed reading of Keynes and Sargent only makes the agreement between the two more remarkable'.

6 What the evidence shows

To test RE is to encounter many substantial difficulties. For instance, the joint REH-NRH hypothesis must be tested and it is difficult to decompose the underlying econometrical structural characteristics of the model from its expectations' mechanism. In addition, most tests involve models which embody price-clearing assumptions.

Sargent (1973(b)) has tested the joint REH-NRH hypothesis and found it was rejected. More recently, after modifying the first test, he found that the narrow version of RE is 'not obscenely at variance with the data' (Sargent, 1976, p. 233). Sargent (1976) and Sargent and Wallace's (1975) later tests brought no conclusive proof in favour of the joint hypothesis. Pesaran (1982) criticizes Barro's (1981 (b and c)) tests of the joint REH-NRH assumption and finds that his specification does not reject the Keynesian hypothesis. Driscoll (1983 (a and b)) develops a model similar to Barro's (1981(b)) and also finds that the joint hypothesis is rejected.

Testing is further thwarted by identification problems and by the fact that the evidence does not reject the traditional, Keynesian adaptive view of the formation of expectations. This is referred to as the 'observational equivalence' problem. For every RE model we can find a non-RE model which fits the data just as well. If the data cannot discriminate between the models, they are called observationally equivalent. Boschen and Grossman (1982, p. 330) test the equilibrium approach to modelling business cycles and conclude that results

> indicate that equilibrium theorizing does not provide an alternative explanation of macroeconomic fluctuations whose implications accord with the apparent facts. The business cycle, consequently, seems mysterious. We do not have at present a theory of fluctuations in aggregate output and employment that is consistent both with maximizing behavior and econometric evidence.

Some economists have tried direct testing – asking people what they expect (for instance, Pesando, 1975). The empirical approach did not at first receive high acclaim from economists nor has it yielded definitive results, but it is growing in popularity. Benjamin Friedman (1980) tested interest rate expectations directly and found evidence unfavourable to RE. Aiginger (1983, 1981 and 1979) also finds discouraging evidence with respect to the REH. Pesaran (1987: book) stresses the importance of the direct measurement of expectations to be used as data in empirical studies.

In a paper which is highly recommended reading for all economists,

Lovell has considered the cumulative empirical evidence found in the literature, concluding that 'the weight of empirical evidence is sufficiently strong to compel us to suspend belief in the hypothesis of rational expectations, pending the accumulation of additional empirical evidence' (1986, p. 122). He recommends (1) that economists consider the full range of expectations formation when conducting empirical research; that they do *not* assume *a priori* that expectations are rational; (2) that the REH be tested against its alternatives, and (3) that models be developed to determine how robust policy conclusions are to departures from expectational rationality.

7 Conclusions

As the 1980s began, Frank Hahn (1983, p. 924) predicted that 'in ten years' time the [rational expectations] "revolution" will be seen to have been a little local disturbance'. As the same decade was coming to a close, however, Mankiw (1988, p. 447) proclaimed that the 'notion of rational expectations is no longer controversial among macroeconomists'. At this juncture in the development of the rational expectations movement, it is still easiest to explain what RE have not been. Although the assumptions of the new classical economists lead to policy neutrality results, none of the versions of the REH necessarily precludes a role for stabilization policy. By advancing more general models, the neutrality result vanishes. Even Lucas prefers

> to stress as the contribution of his papers (1972, 1973) the construction of plausible models of the business cycle based on competitive maximizing behavior and tends to deemphasize the policy implications analyzed by Sargent and Wallace (Lucas, 1981: book, p. 506).

The chapter in which RE and policy neutrality were equated is thus closed.

The REH has indeed transformed macroeconomics and time-series econometric methods. It has caused a change in thinking about the invariance of the structural parameters of mainstream macro models (the Lucas critique) which must be judged as a realistic improvement over existing methods of model building. It has reminded us of the significance of Austrian economics, with its emphasis on expectations and uncertainty, optimization, rationality, Pareto optimality and, especially, on the role of information in economics.

Because the REH was first introduced embedded in a new classical model with policy neutrality conclusions, it is little wonder that the REH school came under scathing attack. Struthers (1984, p. 1150) reaches the conclusion that the usefulness of the new classical models is limited to 'pedagogic lessons': it has caused economists to think through expectations, and it has helped them better to understand Friedman's views. In an impressive book which discusses the limits of the narrow version of RE, Pesaran similarly concludes 'the rational expectations hypothesis, and the adaptive expectations hypothesis that preceded it, represent two different extremes, both of which are based on untenable assumptions and are empirically unsatisfactory' (1987, book: xiv). John Taylor (1982) also

42

argues that traditional Keynesian and new classical views of expectation formation are both too extreme.

Although the narrow form of the REH has run into serious difficulties because of its extreme assumptions, it may still be useful in analysing financial and foreign markets which are believed to display extreme price flexibility and continuous market-clearing properties. (In stock markets the REH is known as the 'efficient markets hypothesis'.) As Shaw argues (1987, p. 204), 'the usefulness of the doctrine depends upon its applications. Clearly, its potential application is greater the simpler the underlying process to be understood and the less demanding is the relevant information set.'

Without doubt a more generalized version of the REH is here to stay. It is, after all, most often the common-sense definition of the generalized version of RE which has been invoked when the narrower forms of RE have been attacked. To summarize the legacy of the REH school: it has raised economists' consciousness of the importance of the role of information and of incorporating expectations into models rather than holding them constant, especially in an inflationary environment.

Notes

1. Myrdal, Gunnar (1969), *Objectivity in Social Research*, New York: Pantheon Books.
2. Gordon, Donald F. (1976), 'A Neo-Classical Theory of Keynesian Unemployment', in Karl Brunner and Allan H. Meltzer (eds.), *The Phillips Curve and Labor Markets*, Vol. 1 of the Carnegie-Rochester Conferences on Public Policy, a supplementary series to the *Journal of Monetary Economics*, Amsterdam/New York/Oxford: North-Holland, p. 65.
3. McCloskey, Donald N. (1985), *The Rhetoric of Economics*, Madison, Wisconsin: University of Wisconsin Press, p. 87.
4. Grunberg, Emile and Franco Modigliani (1954), 'The Predictability of Social Events', *Journal of Political Economy*, **62** (2), December, 465–78.
5. Holt, Charles C., Franco Modigliani, John F. Muth and Herbert A. Simon (1960), *Planning, Production, Inventories and Work Force*, Englewood Cliffs, NJ: Prentice-Hall.
6. Collander and Guthrie (1980–81, p. 230) explain: 'We define reasonable expectations as those expectations that a representative individual would form, given the information available and the costs of acquiring that information. At any point in time, no one reasonable expectation exists, and one must devise models using a "feel" of reality rather than apply an abstract model to explain reality. This, we would argue, is the essence of post Keynesian theory.'
7. Criticisms of the generalized form do exist. For instance, Gomes (1982, p. 53) refers to it as 'an empty statement'. Barro and Fischer (1976, 'Recent Developments in Monetary Theory', *Journal of Monetary Economics*, **2**, p. 163) also remark: 'A fundamental difficulty with theories of expectations that are not based on the predictions of the relevant economic models (rational

expectations) is that they require a theory of systematic mistakes. Such theories are inherently more difficult to formulate that those based on rational behavior, and it seems to be a reasonable strategy to try to do without them.'

8. Hahn, Frank (1982), 'Reflections on the Invisible Hand', *Lloyds Bank Review*, No. 144, April, p. 12.
9. Rawls, John (1971), *A Theory of Justice*, Cambridge, MA: Belknap Press, p. 417.
10. Zero profits are guaranteed by the arbitrage process; profits will always be exploited.
11. Arrow, Kenneth J. (1978), 'The Future and the Present in Economic Life', *Economic Inquiry*, **16**, April, 157–69.
12. *Ibid*, p. 164.
13. Quoted in Robert W. Clower (1969), 'The Keynesian Counter-Revolution: A Theoretical Appraisal', in his *Monetary Theory*, Baltimore: Penguin Books, p. 276.
14. Arrow (1978), p. 169.
15. Hahn (1982), p. 10. There is double definitional muddling here. As Tobin (1980. p. 976) points out, ' "market" is one of the most overworked and imprecise words in economics. Sometimes it is just a figure of speech for voluntary transactions however and wherever consummated. Sometimes it refers to organized exchanges with specific definitions of commodities and established rules. In economic theory it is often just an abstraction, the Walrasian auctioneer that effortlessly and timelessly solves the simultaneous equations to arrive at the market-clearing prices at which all transactions occur.'

    'Clearing' is equally nebulous. It may mean: (a) automatic, rapid adjustment of wages and prices by any method; (b) tâtonnement, or Walrasian adjustment, due to the presence of a fictitious auctioneer; (c) supply adjustments to meet demand; or (d) recontracting or the hypothetical resale of commodities as a process for establishing equilibrium (sometimes also called tâtonnement). An excellent discussion of Say's principle, Walras' law, the equating of supply and demand, etc. is in Robert Clower and Axel Leijonhufvud's (1973), 'Say's Principle, What It Means and Doesn't Mean: Part I', *Intermountain Economic Review*, **4** (2), Fall, 1–16 (Part II never appeared). Reprinted in Axel Leijonhufvud (1981), *Information and Coordination: Essays in Macroeconomic Theory*, New York/Oxford: Oxford University Press, 79–101. Fritz Machlup's (1967) *Essays in Economic Semantics*, New York: Norton and Co. is recommended reading on the subject of sloppy concepts and usage in economics.
16. The traditional concept of a Phillips curve changes in a new classical model: hence the quotation marks.

    Some useful surveys of inflation literature include: Robert J. Gordon (1976), 'Recent Developments in the Theory of Inflation and Unemployment', *Journal of Monetary Economics*, **2**, April, 185–219; 'Inflation Symposium', *Scottish Journal of Political Economy*, **23** (1), February 1976; David Laidler and Michael Parkin (1975), 'Inflation: A Survey', *Economic Journal*, **85** (340), December, 741–809; Arthur M. Okun (1975), 'Inflation: Its Mechanics and Welfare Costs', *Brookings Papers on Economic Activity*, **2**, 351–401; Edmund S. Phelps (1967), 'Phillips Curves, Expectations of Inflation and

Optimal Unemployment over Time', *Economica*, **34** (135), August, 254–81; Anthony M. Santomero and John J. Seater (1978), 'The Inflation-Unemployment Trade-Off: A Critique of the Literature', *Journal of Economic Literature*, **16** (2), June, 499–544.

17. The new classical school's major figures are Robert Barro, Robert Hall, Finn Kydland, Robert Lucas, Bennett McCallum, Thomas Muench, Thomas J. Sargent and Neil Wallace.

18. Friedman, Milton (1968), 'The Role of Monetary Policy', *American Economic Review*, **58** (1), March, 1–17 and Edmund S. Phelps (1967), 'Phillips Curves, Expectations of Inflation and Optimal Unemployment over Time', *Economica*, **34** (135), August, 254–81.

19. Friedman (1968), p. 8.

20. Friedman (1968), p. 11.

21. The name 'disequilibrium theory' is another muddled term as well as a misnomer, often used interchangeably with the term 'non-market-clearing theory'. It does not mean 'not in equilibrium' as the prefix 'dis–' would seem to suggest. Equilibria do occur. Disequilibrium analysis is often associated with wage-price stickiness, but Barro and others have defined it as the non-execution of some perceived and actual mutually advantageous trades'. See Robert Barro (1977), 'Long-Term Contracting, Sticky Prices, and Monetary Policy', *Journal of Monetary Economics*, **3**, p. 315. Barro continues on the same page: 'The non-market-clearing model focuses on fluctuations in the quantity of perceived mutually advantageous trades that are not executed, while market clearing concentrates on fluctuations in the size of the gap between perceived and actual mutually advantageous trades as influenced by imperfect information, stochastic shocks, etc. It is clear from this distinction that first, the two approaches are not logically mutually exclusive, and second, they are distinguished on more than semantic grounds.'

    For current discussions of disequilibrium theory see: Allan Drazen (1980), 'Recent Developments in Macroeconomic Disequilibrium Theory', *Econometrica*, **48** (2), March, 283–306; Frank Hahn (1978), 'On Non-Walrasian Equilibria', *Review of Economic Studies*, **45** (139), February, 1–17; and Peter Howitt (1979), 'Evaluating the Non-Market-Clearing Approach', *American Economic Review*, **69** (2), May, 60–63.

22. I have in mind Friedman, 1968; later works of Friedman, and works of E. S. Phelps.

23. Sometimes authors refer to this as the superneutrality result: 'super' because even in the short run systematic monetary policy loses its effectiveness. However, most often the term is used to refer to the invariance of real variables under different proportional growth rates of the nominal money stock. See Jeremy J. Siegel (1983), 'Technological Change and the Superneutrality of Money', *Journal of Money, Credit, and Banking*, **15** (3), August, 363–7, and in the articles in Part II below, including David Begg (1980).

24. Robertson, Sir Denis (1954), 'Thoughts on Meeting Some Important Persons', *Quarterly Journal of Economics*, **68** (2), May, p. 189.

25. Preston, Alan and Adrian Pagan (1982), *The Theory of Economic Policy: Statistics and Dynamics*, New York: Cambridge University Press, pp. 292–3.

26. Begg's perfect foresight path refers to a situation in which the entire future path of the economy is incorporated into the forecast.

27. See note 23 above.

28. Barro, Robert J. (1974), 'Are Government Bonds Net Wealth', *Journal of Political Economy*, November–December, 1095–1117.
29. This idea has a long history. Consider Schumpeter's references to 'waves of optimism' in his 1939 *Business Cycles: A Theoretical, Historical, and Statistical Analysis of the Capitalist Process* (2 vols). Karl Popper refers to self-fulfilling prophecies which are social policy phenomena such as the 'Oedipus effect', which occur because prediction affects predicted events. See his *Poverty of Historicism*, 2nd ed., 1960.
30. Arrow (1978).
31. Salant, Walter (1969), 'Writing and Reading in Economics', *Journal of Political Economy*, **77** (4), July–August, 545–58.
32. Gordon, Robert A. (1976), 'Rigor and Relevance in a Changing Institutional Setting', *American Economic Review*, **66** (1), p. 5.
33. McCallum, Bennett T. (1982), 'Macroeconomics After a Decade of Rational Expectations: Some Critical Issues', *Economic Review*, Federal Reserve Bank of Richmond, **68** (6), November–December, 3–12.
34. Arrow (1978); Clower (1969); Robert Gordon (1976), 'Recent Developments in the Theory of Inflation and Unemployment', *Journal of Monetary Economics*, **2**, April, 185–219; Robert Gordon (1981), 'Output Fluctuations and Gradual Price Adjustments', *Journal of Economic Literature*, **19**, June, 493–530; Peter Howitt (1979), 'Evaluating the Non-Market-Clearing Approach', *American Economic Review*, **69** (2), May, 60–63; William Poole (1976), 'Rational Expectations in the Macro Model', *Brookings Papers on Economic Activity*, **2**, 463–505 and 'Comments and Discussion', 506–14.
35. Arrow, Kenneth (1981), 'Real and Nominal Magnitudes in Economics', in Daniel Bell and Irving Crystal (eds.), *The Crisis in Economic Theory*, New York: Basic Books, p. 140.
36. Taylor, John B. (1984), 'Recent Developments in the Theory of Stabilization Policy' in Maurice Bullabon (ed.), *Economic Perspectives: An Annual Survey of Economics*, vol. 3, New York: Harwood Academic Publishers, 69–95.
37. But Clower (1969), p. 278 comments: *'either Walras' law is incompatible with Keynesian economics, or Keynes had nothing fundamentally new to add to orthodox economic theory*. This may seem an unnecessarily brutal way to confront one sacred cow with another. But what other conclusion is possible?'
38. Barro, Robert (1979), 'Second Thoughts on Keynesian Economics', *American Economic Review*, **69**, May, 54–9.

PART II

A
COMPREHENSIVE
ANNOTATED
BIBLIOGRAPHY

1   Books

1   ATTFIELD, C.L.F., D. DEMERY and N.W. DUCK (1985)
Rational Expectations in Macroeconomics: An Introduction to Theory and Evidence
Oxford:
Basil Blackwell Inc.

This book, though mainly aimed at students, is a sophisticated introduction to rational expectations. The three authors treat RE within the context of the general significance of expectations in economics, the REH itself, the REH in a flexible-price macroeconomic model, criticisms of this model, RE and the open economy, econometric issues, empirical results, together with criticism and appraisal of the Lucas and Barro models. In the final two chapters they provide case studies and concluding remarks.

2   BARRO, Robert J. (1981)
Money, Expectations, and Business Cycles: Essays in Macroeconomics
New York, London:
Academic Press

This is a collection of some of Barro's early published works that contributed so significantly to new classical macroeconomics. Many of them discuss RE.

3   BEGG, David K.H. (1982)
The Rational Expectations Revolution in Macroeconomics: Theories and Evidence
Oxford: Philip Allan Publishers Ltd
and Baltimore: Johns Hopkins University Press

Begg's goal is to 'convey the key insights of Rational Expectations analysis to undergraduates, business audiences and Civil Servants' (p. xi). He assumes only elementary knowledge of mathematics and macroeconomics, leaving more difficult material to optional, starred sections. Begg introduces the reader to the concept and the historical treatment of expectations formation in the first two chapters. He then defines RE mathematically. In Chapter 4 econometric properties of the REH are discussed. In Chapter 5, a starred chapter, Begg considers more econometrically sophisticated issues: testing the REH, statistical identification, the Lucas problem, etc. Following this, the natural rate hypothesis and stabilization policy are discussed. In Chapters 8 and 9 aggregate demand and efficient asset markets are reviewed in the light of the REH. In the final chapter Begg summarizes and concludes. This work contains a useful bibliography.

4   BOMHOFF, Eduard Jan (1980)
Inflation, the Quantity Theory and Rational Expectations
Vol. 5 of the *Series in Monetary Economics* edited by Karl Brunner
Amsterdam:
North-Holland

The book opens with a general discussion of the theory of inflation and rational expectations. The next three chapters deal with the quantity theory of money and RE models for the US and the Netherlands. The last chapter discusses structural models and RE.

5   BUSCHER, Herbert S. (1986)
Modelle der neuen klassischen Makroökonomie. Theoretische Darstellung und empirische Ergebnisse
München:
Verlag V. Florenz GmbH

As the title indicates, this book considers new classical macroeconomic models. In the first chapter Buscher discusses the theory of rational expectations. In the second he analyses new classical macro models with RE. In the third chapter the model is extended to include an open economy. The Barro model is treated in Chapter 4 and problems with observation in 5. In Part II empirical evidence for Germany is discussed. The final chapters provide a summary and conclusions.

6   CARTER, Michael and Rodney MADDOCK (1984)
Rational Expectations: Macroeconomics for the 1980s?
London/Basingstoke: Macmillan
and Atlantic Highlands, New Jersey: Humanities Press International

This work, aimed at beginning students, discusses the position of
REH within the history of macroeconomics. Expectations and
demand policies to reduce unemployment are explained. Then the
theory of rational expectations as the answer to the macroeconomic
problems of the 1970s and 1980s is presented. Chapter 5 is a
'counter-attack' against rational expectations. In Chapter 6 testing
is the theme, while Chapter 7 provides a summary and conclusions.

7   FISCHER, Stanley (ed.) (1980)
Rational Expectations and Economic Policy
Chicago/London:
University of Chicago Press

This is a collection of papers and discussion documents presented at
a conference on rational expectations and economic policy spon-
sored by the National Bureau of Economic Research in 1978. Con-
tributors include H. Grossman, Barro and Rush, Blanchard, Shiller,
Kydland and Prescott, Lucas, Fischer, Solow and Poole. Comments
and discussion are by Blinder, R. Gordon, R. Weintraub, McCallum, Parkin, Lindsey, Cagan, C. Nelson, J.L. Pierce, Feldstein, Hall,
J.B. Taylor, Willes, Howitt and Wallace.

8   FISHER, Douglas (1988)
Monetary and Fiscal Policy
London: Macmillan Press
and New York: New York University Press

This work is extensively, though not solely, devoted to RE. Fisher
discusses the natural-rate hypothesis and the Lucas supply function,
then devotes two chapters to the REH. By focusing on policy issues,
policy ineffectiveness becomes central to much of the discussion.

9   FRYDMAN, Roman and Edmund S. PHELPS (eds.) (1983)
**Individual Forecasting and Aggregate Outcomes: 'Rational Expec-
tations' Examined**

Cambridge/London/New York:
Cambridge University Press

This comprises the proceedings of a conference on 'Expectations Formation and Economic Disequilibrium' held at New York University in 1981. Participants were Bray, Bull, Cagan, Calvo, Di Tato, Evans, Frydman, J. Green, Hahn, Kirman, Leijonhufvud, Phelps, Radner, J.B. Taylor and Townsend. Topics discussed were the applicability of the REH in analysis of policy changes, expectational stability, learning, decentralization of markets and RE, convergence to equilibrium and a reconsideration of monetarist and Keynesian theories in light of RE.

10   HÄBERLE, Lothar (1982)
Wirtschaftspolitik bei rationalen Erwartungen. Konsequenzen einer kritischen Analyse der Theorie rationaler Erwartungen für die Wahl wirtschaftspolitischer Strategien
Untersuchungen 9, Institut für Wirtschaftspolitik an der Universität zu Köln
Köln: Institut für Wirtschaftspolitik an der Universität zu Köln

This work is divided into three parts: a description of RE in the strict sense, an assessment of this strict version of RE and a discussion of weak (semirational) expectations. In Part I, Häberle considers expectation formation, the interpretation of RE, a comparison of RE and autoregressive expectation formation, the efficient market theory and policy questions. In Part II he discusses information costs, problems with estimating the model, institutional problems (wage and price rigidity, etc.), empirical evidence and a weak formulation of RE. In Part III he covers learning processes, consequences for policy, unemployment, a comparison of policy centred on tradeoffs and that built on semirational expectations, and a conclusion that expresses reservations and hopes for RE.

11   HOLDEN, K., D.A. PEEL and J.L. THOMPSON (1985)
Expectations: Theory and Evidence
London: Macmillan
and New York: St Martin

Holden, Peel and Thompson intend their work to be an introduction to the theories of expectation formation, with empirical evidence

concerning these theories. The book is geared to advanced undergraduates and graduate students of macroeconomic and monetary
economics. The authors first introduce the reader to expectations
formation and then consider the theory of RE. The third chapter
surveys evidence on expectations formation; the fourth deals with
the efficient markets hypothesis, and the next three discuss econometric aspects, followed by conclusions.

12   HOOVER, Kevin D. (1988)
     The New Classical Macroeconomics: A Sceptical Inquiry
     Oxford and New York:
     Basil Blackwell

This book is not devoted to rational expectations, but to new classical economics which was originally – and wrongly – equated with
rational expectations. The five-part book considers the following
topics respectively: RE; new classical analyses of the labour market
and business cycles; new classical monetary and fiscal policy; econometric issues associated with new classical economics; and method-
ological issues (a comparison of new classical economics with monetarism and Austrian economics). This book is highly recommended
for its critical insights.

13   KLAMER, Arjo (1984)
     **The New Classical Macroeconomics: Conversations with the New
     Classical Economists and Their Opponents**
     Brighton: Wheatsheaf Books Ltd
     and Totowa, NJ: Rowman & Allanheld

Klamer interviews Lucas, Sargent and Townsend (proponents of the
new classical economics); Tobin, Modigliani and Solow (the older
generation of neo-Keynesians); Blinder and J.B. Taylor (the new
generation of neo-Keynesians); Brunner (monetarist); and D. Gordon and Rapping (nonconventional economists). In the final
chapter he interprets the conversations, concluding that rhetoric
(style, how something is said) is the source of their disagreements.

14   KLAUSINGER, Hansjörg (1980)
     Rationale Erwartungen und die Theorie der Stabilisierungspolitik

Bern/Frankfurt am Main/Las Vegas:
Peter Lang

As the title indicates, this work focuses on RE and stabilization policy. First Klausinger discusses the theoretical foundation of stabilization policy. Then he describes macro models, the new classical economics and the concept of RE. In the third chapter he deals with stabilization policy and RE. Finally he considers RE macro models and contracts, equilibrium with RE, optimal stabilization policy and RE, empirical tests and problems with and critique of RE.

15 KÜHN, Bruno (1979)
Rationale Erwartungen und Wirtschaftspolitik
Baden-Baden:
Nomos Verlagsgesellschaft

This book also considers policy questions. In the first two chapters Kühn discusses the controversy surrounding the Phillips curve – the environment from which the RE school sprang. He explores inflation and unemployment, the formation of all types of expectations, monetary policy and contracts. In the final chapter he assesses the practical significance of RE and discusses business-cycle policy.

16 LAHIRI, Kajal (1981)
The Econometrics of Inflationary Expectations
Vol. 7, *Studies in Monetary Economics*
Amsterdam/New York/Oxford:
North-Holland Publishing Co.

This work does not deal exclusively with RE, but considers related topics such as the Phillips curve and efficient markets. Chapter 3 deals with RE in macro models, while Chapter 5 studies RE and the Fisher effect.

17 LUCAS, Robert E. (1987)
Models of Business Cycles
Oxford and Cambridge, MA:
Basil Blackwell

In this slim volume Lucas develops a RE model of the Kydland-

Prescott type which he believes is valuable for business-cycle research. He then discusses unemployment and monetary considerations as well as monetary disturbances. In the final chapter Lucas sums up the ramifications of the theory for policy-making.

18 LUCAS, Robert E. Jr (1981)
Studies in Business Cycle Theory
Cambridge, MA/London, England:
MIT Press

Fourteen of Lucas' papers on business cycles written between 1967 and 1980 are brought together in this volume. These papers form a vital part of the framework of the new classical school of economics.

19 LUCAS, Robert E. and Thomas J. SARGENT (eds.) (1981)
Rational Expectations and Econometric Practice
London: George Allen and Unwin
and Minneapolis: University of Minnesota Press

This thick volume brings together some important papers on RE written by Muth, Sargent, Lucas, L.P. Hansen, Prescott, Wallace, Barro, Fischer, McCallum, Wallis, Chow, Granger, Sims, Hall, Kydland, Calvo and J.B. Taylor. Lucas and Sargent provide an introduction which relates the papers one to another.

20 LÜBBERS, Ralf (1981)
Inflation, Beschäftigung und rationale Erwartungen
Berlin:
Duncker & Humblot

'Inflation, Employment and Rational Expectations' centres on the Phillips curve relationship and controversy. First Lübbers discusses the empirical relationship between inflation, relative prices and employment. He then describes the Phillips curve in alternative macro models and how expectations and macro models of non-Walrasian behaviour are formed. Finally he analyses an equilibrium model with RE and offers a conclusion.

21   MACESICH, George (1987)
     Monetary Policy and Rational Expectations
     New York/Westport, CN/London:
     Praeger

This book, written for the general economist, students and laymen, is not rigorous. The work concerns the importance of expectations in the formulation of monetary policy. Monetarists, new classicism, business cycles and empirical evidence are all considered in relation to RE.

22   MINFORD, Patrick and David PEEL (1983)
     Rational Expectations and the New Macroeconomics
     Oxford: Martin Robertson
     and Cambridge, MA: Basil Blackwell

This is an intermediate and rather unusual introduction to RE. After an introductory chapter, the authors show how RE models are solved and then discuss stabilization policy. The rest of the work considers issues not normally tackled: the effects of partial information, problems in choosing optimal policies, the Phillips curve given RE, efficient asset markets, the political economy of democracy, wealth effects and bond-financed deficits, the problem of observational equivalence and the Liverpool model.

23   MISHKIN, Frederic S. (1983)
     A Rational Expectations Approach to Macroeconomics: Testing Policy Ineffectiveness and Efficient-Markets Models
     Chicago:
     University of Chicago Press

The subject of the first part of this book is the method of rational expectations within an econometrics framework together with tests of rationality. In the second part Mishkin discusses the rationality of market forecasts, monetary policy and interest rates, as well as the policy ineffectiveness issue. In the final chapter he comments favourably on the RE approach.

24   PERSSON, Mats (1979)
     Inflationary Expectations and the Natural Rate Hypothesis

Stockholm:
The Economic Research Institute at the Stockholm School of Economics

The first part of this book reviews the theory of stochastic processes (time series analysis, ARMA processes, stationarity). Then Persson discusses the formation of expectations in macro models and – in a particularly useful section – compares adaptive and rational expectations. He concludes that rational expectations are not rational because they have no solid micro foundations.

25 PESARAN, M. Hashem (1987)
The Limits to Rational Expectations
Oxford/New York:
Basil Blackwell

Pesaran's work is a critical, highly technical assessment of the REH. The author discusses the nature and sources of uncertainty; the problems of information heterogeneity, learning and information acquisition; and the non-uniqueness of the solution to RE models with future expectations. The book deals with the contributions made from econometrics, with the identification of linear RE models, and with estimation and hypothesis testing in these models. In the final part measurement of expectations, direct tests of the REH, and models of expectation formation under bounded rationality are discussed. He concludes with the assertion in Chapter 10 that the strong version of the REH (advanced by Muth) is not always realistic. Since the most important issue surrounding the REH is the learning problem, Pesaran suggests that an integrated approach to learning and expectations formation should be taken. In five appendices, he summarizes the statistical/mathematical background information related to the REH and provides substantial data.

26 PRECIOUS, Mark (1987)
Rational Expectations, Nonmarket Clearing, and Investment Theory
Oxford/New York/Toronto/Melbourne:
Oxford University Press, Clarendon Press

Precious examines investment theory in the light of rational expectations and disequilibrium theory. First the author reviews theories of investment (postwar theories, Keynesian investment theory, and a Jorgenson-Keynes mix) and then considers the q theory and market non-clearing. In the final chapters Precious presents a q model of investment extended to take into account disequilibrium in the goods and labour markets. Lastly he discusses sales and employment constraints as well as investment within a RE model.

27   RIBHEGGE, Hermann (1987)
Grenzen der Theorie rationaler Erwartungen. Zur wirtschaftspolitischen Bedeutung rationaler Erwartungen auf walrasianischen und nicht–walrasianischen Märkten
Vol. 49 of *Die Einheit der Gesellschaftswissenschaften. Studien in den Grenzbereichen der Wirtschafts- und Sozialschaften*
Tübingen:
J.C.B. Mohr

This work analyses the significance of various factors including expectations for business cycle theory; expectations in Walrasian equilibrium models; variations in RE and in stability conclusions; the RE assumption; expectations in non-Walrasian models; the influence of the money supply on price levels and employment in alternative market forms; and, finally, indeterminacy in multimarket models and its effect on an anticipated change in money supply.

28   SARGENT, Thomas J. (1987)
Macroeconomic Theory, 2nd ed.
Boston/New York/London:
Academic Press, Inc.

Part II of this work is devoted to stochastic macroeconomics. The techniques described in these chapters must be mastered if the reader is fully to understand RE. The book teaches 'the language of applied macroeconomics' (xxi): behaviour under uncertainty, difference equations and lag operators, and linear least square projections and linear stochastic difference equations. Other chapters consider applications: implicit labour contracts and sticky wages, the consumption function, government debt and taxes, investment under uncertainty, dynamic optimal taxation, the Phillips curve, optimal monetary policy and the new classical macroeconomics.

29 SARGENT, Thomas (1986)
    Rational Expectations and Inflation
    New York:
    Harper and Row

Compared to the previous entry, this is an elementary exposition of
the nature of RE, with a strong policy orientation. Sargent builds a
RE model in Chapter 1. He then proceeds to analyse Reaganomics,
the four 'big' inflations (Germany, Austria, Hungary, Poland), as
well as Poincaré and Thatcher economics. Chapter 5, 'Some
Unpleasant Monetarist Arithmetic', was written with Neil Wallace
and concentrates on the theme that monetary and fiscal policy are
interrelated and must therefore be coordinated. The final chapter is
a case study of Hong Kong.

30 SCHILLING, Günter (1987)
    Rationale Erwartungen in makroökonomischen Modellen
    St Gallen:
    Verlag Wilhelm Surbir

Schilling first discusses expectations in an historical perspective.
Then various themes are considered: expectations hypotheses, equilibrium and RE, the standard model, RE in disequilibrium models,
and criticism of the assumptions of the new classical economics.

31 SHAW, George Keith (1984)
    Rational Expectations: An Elementary Exposition
    Brighton: Wheatsheaf Books
    and New York: St Martin

This is an elementary work for students, demanding only the most
basic knowledge of economics and mathematics. In the first six
chapters (and with the help of numerous examples) Shaw develops
the idea of RE, the natural rate hypothesis and the business cycle.
He then sets out the role of RE with respect to price flexibility,
econometrics and fiscal policy. His final chapter is dedicated to an
assessment and critique of RE. Included is a bibliography and
suggestions for further reading.

32   SHEFFRIN, Steven M. (1983)
     Rational Expectations
     Cambridge/London/New York:
     Cambridge University Press

This, again, is an intermediate-level introduction to RE. After explaining the concept, he discusses its relevance for inflation, unemployment and econometrics. Further topics include efficient markets and RE, microeconomic models, and the impact of RE on macroeconomics and policy.

33   SIJBEN, J.J. (1980)
     Rational Expectations and Monetary Policy
     Alphen aan den Rijn: Sijthoff & Noordhoff
     and Norwell, MA: Kluwer Academic

Monetary policy and expectations in retrospect are discussed. The Phillips curve, the REH and a critical review of the RE theory follow.

34   WHITEMAN, Charles H. (1983)
     Linear Rational Expectation Models: A User's Guide
     Minneapolis:
     University of Minnesota Press

Whiteman sets forth a guide to understanding and solving stationary linear RE models where the solution is a particular sort of fixed point.

2 Articles

35 ABEL, Andrew B. and Frederic MISHKIN (1983)
'An Integrated View of Tests of Rationality, Market Efficiency and the Short-Run Neutrality of Monetary Policy'
Journal of Monetary Economics, **11** (1): 3–24

The authors test rationality, capital market efficiency and the short-run neutrality of monetary policy, pointing out the common elements of the tests.

36 ADOLPH, Brigitte and Elmar WOLFSTETTER (1985)
'Pareto-verbessernde Fiskalpolitik im allgemeinen Gleichgewicht bei rationalen Erwartungen'
Zeitschrift für Wirtschafts- und Sozialwissenschaften, **105** (1): 51–63

This work presents a general equilibrium, rational expectations model with an incomplete set of markets (that is, without insurance markets). The existing markets always clear. Despite this, the market does not exhibit Pareto-efficient employment and risk-sharing unless shocks are purely of the monetary type, a situation interpreted in terms of welfare concepts. Pareto improvements are suggested.

37 AIGINGER, Karl (1983)
'Die Wirkung von asymmetrischen Verlusten auf die Bildung von rationalen ökonomischen Erwartungen' ('The Incorporation of Asymmetric Losses into the Formation of Economically Rational Expectations')
Ifo-Studien, **29** (3): 175–215

The author argues that loss evaluations should be incorporated into expectations. He shows that these losses are asymmetric for different errors in expectations. When both conditions obtain, rational expectations will not equal realizations even in the long run.

38   AIGINGER, Karl (1981)
      'Empirical Evidence on the Rational Expectations Hypothesis Using
      Reported Expectations'
      Empirica, 1: 25–72

      The goal of the paper is to test rational against actual expectations.
      When using empirically measured expectations, the honesty of the
      reports is questionable. The evidence does not favour rational
      expectations. The author admits, however, that there may be errors
      in measuring expectations. Moreover, confronting realizations with
      expectations is only one approach to testing rationality.

39   AIGINGER, K. (1979)
      'Mean, Variance and Skewness of Reported Expectations and Their
      Differences to the Respective Moments of Realizations'
      Empirica, 2 (2): 217–65

      Despite the assumption that expectations are not measurable, Aig-
      inger contends that considerable data on expectations do exist and
      can be matched against realizations. Aiginger discovers that the
      expectations deviate from the realizations, the former tending to fall
      short of the latter.

40   AKERLOF, G.A. (1979)
      'The Case Against Conservative Macroeconomics: An Inaugural
      Lecture'
      Economica, 46 (183), August: 219–37

      Akerlof defends Keynesian against new classical economics. He
      questions the new classical conclusion that fiscal policy is impotent
      and attacks the realism of the assumptions behind the Sargent
      models.

41   ALBERRO, Jose (1980)
      'The Lucas Hypothesis on the Phillips Curve: Further International
      Evidence'
      Journal of Monetary Economics, 7 (2), October: 239–50

      The author tests the Lucas hypothesis on the Phillips curve by
      making cross-country comparisons. Lucas' hypothesis posits that

nominal shocks affect the cyclical component of real aggregates if agents mistake them for movements in real variables. Alberro finds that the Lucas hypothesis on the Phillips curve is confirmed: a negative relation exists between output and inflation and the unpredictability of exogenous shocks.

42　ALLEN, Beth (1985a)
'The Existence of Fully Rational Expectations Approximate Equilibria with Noisy Price Observations'
Journal of Economic Theory, **37** (2), December: 213–53

In this work the author assumes that prices transmit some information from informed to uninformed traders, but that they do not carry all of the available information. Her main conclusion is that fully rational expectations approximate equilibria exist when agents condition their expected utilities on the equilibrium price function, on their own noisy price observations, and on the distributions of noisy price observations. In that case, total excess demand is very small, with high probability. The expected discrepancy from exact market clearing is also very small for every state of the world.

43　ALLEN, Beth (1985b)
'The Existence of Rational Expectations Equilibria in a Large Economy with Noisy Price Observations'
Journal of Mathematical Economics, **14** (1): 67–103

The author argues that non-revealing expectations exist in microeconomic pure exchange economies where a continuum of uninformed agents have suitably distributed noisy price observations. The key condition for continuity and smoothness of aggregate excess demand is slight dispersion of prices. Equilibria occur in markets which approximately clear and are obtained by applying a fixed-point argument to state-dependent excess demand functions.

44　ALLEN, Beth (1983)
'Expectations Equilibria with Dispersed Information: Existence with Approximate Rationality in a Model with a Continuum of Agents and Finitely Many States of the World'
Review of Economic Studies, **50** (2), April: 267–85

Allen presents a model of a large economy in which prices transmit information about the state of the world from more-informed to less-informed agents. Assuming that the forecast functions of imperfectly-informed agents are suitably dispersed, she finds that for any such distribution of forecasts, market clearing prices do exist: there is always an equilibrium in which each agent's expectations are approximately rational.

45   ALLEN, Beth (1982a)
'Approximate Equilibria in Microeconomic Rational Expectations Models'
Journal of Economic Theory, **26** (2), April: 244–60

In this paper Allen weakens the definition of equilibrium (permitting markets which only approximately clear) to allow the existence of rational expectations. With approximate market clearing, the existence of RE approximate equilibria requires only a compactness condition. This is a second-best solution to the nonexistence (of exact equilibria) problem.

46   ALLEN, Beth (1982b)
'Strict Rational Expectations Equilibria with Diffuseness'
Journal of Economic Theory, **27** (1), June: 20–46

Allen shows that a diffuseness condition on the distribution of traders' characteristics exists for smooth state pure exchange economies under uncertainty when the state of the world varies, permitting the use of only a weak dimensionality restriction in the proof of the existence of RE.

47   ALLSBROOK, Ogden O. Jr (1986)
'Rational Expectations and Crowding-Out'
Kredit und Kapital, **19** (2): 248–51

The author casts the REH into an IS-LM framework and considers the effects of monetary policy. He finds that crowding out occurs.

48   ALOGOSKOUFIS, George S. and John NISSIM (1981)
'Consumption-Income Dynamics Under Rational Expectations: Theory and Evidence'

Greek Economic Review, **3** (2), August: 128–47

The paper offers a model of consumption based on habit persistence. Current, not permanent, income drives the decisions of households. Expectations are rational. The short-run income elasticity of consumption was found to be 0.4.

49 ALOGOSKOUFIS, George S. and C.A. PISSARIDES (1983)
'A Test of Price Sluggishness in the Simple Rational Expectations Model: UK 1950–1980'
Economic Journal, **93** (371), September: 616–28

The author argues that observed lagged responses of prices and output to changes in nominal variables may or may not be consistent with the neutrality proposition of the RE new classical models. Whether they are consistent or not depends on the source of the observed lags and on the rules used to determine output.

50 ANDERSON, Paul A. (1979)
'Rational Expectations from Nonrational Models'
Journal of Monetary Economics, **5** (1), January: 67–80

The author presents simulation results from two large-scale econometric models that incorporate the Lucas critique and the REH. Anderson provides a method for simulating standard models with the additional assumption of RE when re-estimation is considered to be too costly. He argues that the results of the RE simulations indicate that the Lucas critique is of great importance for econometric policy evaluation.

51 ANDERSON, R.M. and H. SONNENSCHEIN (1985)
'Rational Expectations Equilibrium with Econometric Models'
Review of Economic Studies, **52** (3), July: 359–69

In this paper the authors prove the existence of general equilibrium under uncertainty; in other words, the state of the environment is random. Economic agents receive private information correlated with the state of the environment, but prices are public. Hence each agent receives more than private information about the state of the environment. Prices then play an allocative role as well as transferring information. The authors show there is at least 1 RE equilibrium for each n-agent economy in a general class.

52   AOKI, Masanao and Matthew CANZONERI (1979)
      'Reduced Forms of Rational Expectations Models'
      Quarterly Journal of Economics, **93** (1), February: 59–71

The goal of this paper is to generalize Muth's original 1961 method of deriving reduced-form equations of a model which is applicable to macroeconomics. This method should work for any linear RE model with rational means, variances and higher moments. Deriving reduced forms for a large number of RE models in this class, the authors formulate a rule for specifying valid reduced-form structures for all of them.

53   ASAKO, Kazumi (1982)
      'Rational Expectations and the Effectiveness of Monetary Policy with Special Reference to the Barro-Fisher Model'
      Journal of Monetary Economics, **9** (1) January: 99–107

The main purpose of this paper is to show that the new classical conclusion of the ineffectiveness of monetary policy is not a generalized result. Asako proves that this holds only because the money supply changes follow a specific rule, namely a random walk.

54   ATESOGLU, H. Sonmez and Donald DUTKOWSKY (1984)
      'Rational Expectations, Fatality, and Keynesian Models'
      Quarterly Journal of Business and Economics, **23** (3), Summer: 18–28

The authors compare a Keynesian IS-LM model with a rational expectations model and determine that each provides a satisfactory explanation of prices and output in the 1970s. They indicate that combining the two approaches may be fruitful in business fluctuation research.

55   ATTFIELD, C.L.F. and Martin J. BROWNING (1985)
      'A Differential Demand System, Rational Expectations and the Life Cycle Hypothesis'
      Econometrica, **53** (1), January: 31–48

The life cycle-rational expectations hypothesis maintains that consumers allocate expenditures across time in such a way that the marginal utility of money follows a random walk. The authors present estimates of a demand system within this framework. Their results do not support the REH. Nonetheless their estimates are sensible, suggesting that further research on these lines is warranted.

56   AUTUME, Antoine d' (1986)
'Les anticipations rationnelles dans l'analyse macro-économique'
('Rational Expectations and Macroeconomic Analysis')
Revue économique, **37** (2), March: 243–83

This article reviews RE and the new classical literature, outlining the characteristics of the latter school. A Sargent-Wallace model, a general new classical and a simple new classical model are examined. Then the foundations of new classical economics are discussed, including equilibrium, IS-LM, and both the absence of superneutrality and the multiplicity of solutions in a plausible model. Finally, new classical economics and traditional monetarism, political economy and new classicism, and macroeconometric models are analysed. Conclusions are offered.

57   AZARIADIS, Costas (1981)
'Self-Fulfilling Prophecies'
Journal of Economic Theory, **25** (3): 380–96

Here 'extraneous uncertainty' is found to be frequent among rational expectations equilibria in an aggregative model of overlapping generations. Azariadis gives examples of fulfilling prophecies corresponding to a permanent boom or recession in an economy entirely free of price rigidities. This raises the possibility that business cycles are elicited by arbitrary shifts in anything – no matter how purely subjective – and thus that price changes signal no structural information in such cases.

58   AZARIADIS, Costas and Russell COOPER (1985)
'Nominal Wage Price Rigidity as a Rational Expectations Equilibrium'
American Economic Review, **75** (2), May: 31–35

The authors discuss examples of intertemporal economies with RE equilibria in which wages and prices are predetermined, output is sensitive to policy shocks, and markets are cleared. Then Nash equilibria are considered when producers set prices and wages. Contracts are not found to be necessary for the existence of equilibria with predetermined wages and prices. Moreover, predetermined wage and price equilibria do not exist if policy is too variable.

59   BACKUS, David and John DRIFFILL (1985)
'Rational Expectations and Policy Credibility Following a Change in Regime'
Review of Economic Studies, **52** (2), April: 211–21

The dynamic path of an economy following a change in policy is analysed. Both the new policy and the public's reaction to it are unknown. The authors apply Kreps and Wilson's reputation model to Barro and Gordon's macroeconomic policy game. Equilibrium represents the solution to the game between the government and private sector. Mixed strategies and learning occur on both sides until uncertainties about the new policy are resolved. The model developed by Backus and Driffill illustrates the credibility problem facing a government when the public is sceptical of its motives.

60   BAILLIE, Richard, Robert E. LIPPENS and Patrick C. MCMAHON (1983)
'Testing Rational Expectations and Efficiency in the Foreign Exchange Market'
Econometrica, **51** (3), May: 553–63

The authors test the hypothesis that the forward exchange rate is an unbiased predictor of the future spot rate. The hypothesis is rejected. This could mean either that the REH is wrong or that the assumption of neutrality is unfounded.

61   BANKS, Jeffrey (1985)
'Price-Conveyed Information Versus Observed Insider Behavior: A Note on Rational Expectations Convergence'
Journal of Political Economy, **93** (4): 807–15

In this comment Banks repeats Plott and Sunder's (1982) experiment, altering the information structure. He is able to confirm Plott and Sunder's conclusions regarding price dynamics of the market, but not the claim that uninformed traders learn the state of the market from the market price.

62   BARRO, Robert J. (1984)
'What Survives of the Rational Expectations Revolution? Rational Expectations and Macroeconomics in 1984'
American Economic Review: Papers and Proceedings, **74** (2), May: 179–82

The nature of this paper is reflective rather than expository. Barro argues that the 'rational' sense of rational expectations has been accepted by most economists; in other words, that people use information to form their expectations and are motivated to acquire information. He adds, however, that research has not yielded definitive answers on the nonneutrality of money or on the business cycle in general. He proceeds to discuss areas of potential fruitful research.

63   BARRO, Robert J. (1981a)
'Rational Expectations and the Role of Monetary Policy'
in Lucas and Sargent, 1981: 229–59
rpt in the *Journal of Monetary Economics*, **2** (1), January 1976: 1–32

Barro examines the role of monetary policy in a model in which markets clear, expectations are rational, prices and quantities are determined in a competitive equilibrium system, and information is imperfect. He concludes that monetary policy is basically in accord with Milton Friedman's proposal for a constant growth rate rule. Only if the monetary authority has superior information should there be a departure from this rule.

64   BARRO, Robert J. (1981b)
'Unanticipated Money Growth and Unemployment in the United States'
in Lucas and Sargent, 1981: 563–84

Barro argues that only anticipated movements in money affect real economic variables like unemployment or output level. In testing this hypothesis, he found that unanticipated money growth also had considerable explanatory value regarding unemployment.

65   BARRO, Robert J. (1981c)
'Unanticipated Money, Output, and the Price Level in the United States'
in Lucas and Sargent, 1981: 585–616

In this analysis Barro extends the project begun in 1981(b), checking the effects of monetary changes on price level and the rate of inflation. He finds support for the hypothesis that anticipated movements in the money stock are reflected in one-to-one contemporaneous movements of the price level.

66   BARRO, Robert (1976)
'Indexation in a Rational Expectations Model'
Journal of Economic Theory, **13** (2), October: 229–44

Indexation has been used to insulate the real economy from monetary disturbances; that is, to eliminate the short-run tradeoff between output and unanticipated inflation (the Phillips curve). Barro develops a model in which indexation operates by producing some *ex post* adjustment of local prices. He finds that indexation has no effect on output but does affect price distributions, increasing the variance of future prices around currently predictable values. Indexation also reduces dispersion of prices across markets.

67   BARRO, Robert J. and Mark RUSH (1980)
'Unanticipated Money and Economic Activity', with comments from A.S. Blinder, R. Gordon and R. Weintraub
in Fischer, 1980: 23–73

This is a discussion of the relation of money to economic activity in post-war US. The distinction between anticipated and unanticipated movements in money is analysed.

68   BAUSOR, Randall (1985)
'Conceptual Evolution in Economics: The Case of Rational Expectations'
Eastern Economic Journal, **11** (4): 297–308

Bausor argues that RE theorists have joined the ideas of rationality and equilibrium in the same term, lending it great appeal to many economists. He elaborates on the role that language plays in the appeal of RE new classical models.

69　BAUSOR, Randall (1983)
'The Rational-Expectations Hypothesis and the Epistemics of Time'
Cambridge Journal of Economics, **7** (1), March: 1–10

Bausor argues that RE do not embody an epistemically historical view of time (that is, one which emphasizes uncertainty). The extreme information assumptions of the new classical models are incompatible with a truly historical analysis.

70　BEGG, David K.H. (1982)
'Rational Expectations, Wage Rigidity and Involuntary Unemployment: A Particular Theory'
Oxford Economic Papers, **34** (1), March: 23–47

Here Begg argues that Keynesianism has been abandoned too quickly in favour of monetarist and RE positions. He offers a model which embraces RE and labour-market microfoundation considerations and is still consistent with Keynesian policy prescriptions. Markets do not clear in the short run and involuntary employment is possible. Individuals form RE. Demand management is effective and recommended.

71　BEGG, David H.K. (1980)
'Rational Expectations and the Non-Neutrality of Systematic Monetary Policy'
Review of Economic Studies, **47** (2), January: 293–303

The goal of this paper is to show that money is not superneutral in a general RE model. The new classical models impose superneutrality; it is not an outcome of the model. Begg analyses the conditions under which money is neutral.

72　BENAVIE, A. (1985)
'Monetary-Fiscal Policy Under Rational Expectations in a Lucas-Rapping Macromodel'
Atlantic Economic Journal, **13** (4), December: 1–9

The focus of this paper is the derivation of a short-run closed macromodel from an expanded Lucas-Rapping framework. The author carries out a comparative static analysis of monetary and fiscal policy under both predetermined and rational expectations. He finds that the Barro supply function emerges from the Lucas-Rapping framework if labour is the only variable input and if taxes and wealth effects on labour supply are ignored. The supply function derived is therefore an extension of Barro's supply function, but it does not allow neutrality to hold.

73   BENAVIE, A. (1983)
'Optimal Monetary Policy Under Rational Expectations with a Micro-Based Supply Function'
Journal of Macroeconomics, **5** (2), Spring: 149–66

This paper examines optimal monetary policy in a typical RE model with an aggregate supply function modified so that it is derived from a two-period, choice-theoretic basis. Benavie finds that a combination policy is optimal for stabilizing output or price if there are random disturbances in the IS curve. Given monetary disturbances, he finds that an interest rate target is optimal for stabilizing both price and output variance, confirming findings in the literature. A combination policy is optimal if the random disturbances are in the aggregate supply curve.

74   BERKMAN, Neil G. (1980)
'A Rational View of Rational Expectations'
New England Economic Review, January–February: 18–29

This is a non-technical article reviewing the impact and meaning of rational expectations in macroeconomics. The policy inefficacy assumption of the new classical models is attacked. Berkman argues that the RE school has nonetheless helped economists better to understand policy issues.

75   BHATTACHARYA, Gautam (1987)
'Notes on Optimality of Rational Expectations Equilibrium with Incomplete Markets'
Journal of Economic Theory, **42** (2), August: 191–208

The author analyses the Pareto optimality properties of RE equilibria in an exchange economy with pre-state security markets and post-state spot markets. It is found that, under certain conditions, RE equilibria can be supported by the market. But nonoptimal equilibria may exist, and the introduction of additional securities may make everyone worse off.

76   BILSON, J.F.O. (1980a)
'The Permanent Income Hypothesis under Rational Expectations'
American Journal of Agricultural Economics, **62** (2), May: 319–24

This is a summary of Bilson's 1980(b) article below.

77   BILSON, J.F.O. (1980b)
'The Rational Expectations Approach to the Consumption Function: A MultiCountry Study'
European Economic Review, **13** (3), May: 273–99

Bilson assesses the implications of the permanent income hypothesis for the estimation of aggregate demand functions. The results generally support the application of the REH to the estimation of demand functions with permanent income.

78   BLACK, Fischer (1974)
'Uniqueness of the Price Level in Monetary Growth Models with Rational Expectations'
Journal of Economic Theory, **7** (1), January: 53–65

Black develops a growth model incorporating RE. He finds that when a new monetary policy is announced, the various combinations of a new price level and rate of inflation encourage individuals to hold their existing stock of real balances. The REH alone does not identify which of the many possible paths the economy could take. Rather, there are multiple competitive equilibria.

79   BLACK, S.W. (1972)
'The Use of Rational Expectations in Models of Speculation'
Review of Economic Statistics, **54** (2), May: 161–5

Black uses Muth's model of RE to derive a dummy variable method of dealing with both unforeseen and foreseen disturbances in situations where speculation is important. He applies his method specifically to international capital movements of the late 1930s.

80   BLAKE, D. (1984)
'Complete Systems Methods of Estimating Models with Rational and Adaptive Expectations: A Case Study'
European Economic Review, **24** (2), March: 137–50

The author compares a model with rational and adaptive expectations using complete systems methods of estimation. He finds that the model (the Stein model) is misspecified; thus he cannot determine whether adaptive or rational expectations is the more appropriate expectations-generating approach to use to model the US economy.

81   BLANCHARD, Olivier Jean (1983)
'Methods of Solution and Simulation for Dynamic Rational Expectations Models'
Economie appliquée, **36** (1): 27–46

The purpose of this paper is to introduce the principle methods for solving dynamic RE models. The fact that they are much more difficult to solve than other dynamic models probably restricts their use.

82   BLANCHARD, Olivier Jean (1980)
'The Monetary Mechanism in the Light of Rational Expectations',
with comments by McCallum, Parkin and Lindsey
in Fischer, 1980: 75–116

Blanchard uses a structural model to examine the effects of anticipated and unanticipated monetary policy given RE. He analyses the effects of policy on output, the short-run interest rate and the stock market. His main aim is to specify a macroeconomic model which can be used for valid policy simulations (that is, one taking into account the Lucas critique).

83   BLANCHARD, Olivier Jean (1979)
'Backward and Forward Solutions for Economies with Rational Expectations'

American Economic Review: Papers and Proceedings, **69** (2), May: 114–18

In models where rational expectations of future endogenous variables influence current behaviour, there are an infinite number of solutions. Finding a unique or 'forward solution' has usually been dealt with by imposing one of three conditions: optimality, consistency of behaviour or stationarity. Blanchard reviews this problem and finds that consistency is unacceptable. The stationarity condition may be justified but does not always guarantee a unique solution. He suggests areas for future research.

84 BLANCHARD, O.J. and Charles M. KAHN (1980)
'The Solution of Linear Difference Models under Rational Expectations'
Econometrica, **48** (5), July: 1305–11

This paper presents the solution to a subclass of the general linear difference RE models. The authors show how the solution is derived and how it can be put into the reduced form. Finally, they provide the reader with the conditions for existence and uniqueness.

85 BLANCHARD, Olivier J. and Mark W. WATSON (1984)
'Bubbles, Rational Expectations, and Financial Markets'
in Paul Wachtel (ed.), *Crises in the Economic and Financial Structure*
Lexington, Mass./Toronto: Lexington Books: 295–315

The authors investigate rational bubbles – when the price of an asset is not equal to its true value (such deviations from true value are, however, rational). They find that bubbles are likely to have real effects on the economy and discuss the myriad difficulties of testing for them.

86 BLINDER, Alan S. (1987)
'Keynes, Lucas, and Scientific Progress'
American Economic Review: Papers and Proceedings, **77** (2), May: 130–36

Blinder uses an entertaining style to describe Lucas' influence on economics from a Keynesian perspective. He answers the following questions: (1) Are expectations rational? (2) Is there involuntary unemployment? (3) Do wage movements quickly clear the labour market? (4) Is the NRU a useful concept? (5) Is there a reliable SR Phillips curve? (6) Does a change in the money supply have real effects? (7) Does social welfare rise when business cycles are dampened? and (8) Does macro have to be built on neoclassical first principles? The answers are, respectively, 1–no; 2–yes; 3–no; 4–no; 5–in the past, yes; 6–yes; 7–yes; 8–no. Lucas' answers are all essentially the opposite. Blinder concludes that Keynesian economics is more scientific than neoclassical economics.

87　BLINDER, Alan S. (1986)
'Keynes After Lucas'
Eastern Economic Journal, **12** (3), July–September: 209–16

Blinder reviews and summarizes the theoretical elements of the Keynesian consensus before RE emerged in the 1970s. He then discusses the developments of RE and assesses the situation in modern macroeconomics.

88　BLINDER, Alan S. (1981)
'Monetary Accommodation of Supply Shocks under Rational Expectations'
Journal of Money, Credit, and Banking, **13** (4), November: 425–38

Blinder augments two models of Lucas and Fischer by introducing an imported intermediate good – oil – which is used as an input for domestic output. He finds an exploitable inflation-employment relationship in the short run where anticipated OPEC shocks are concerned; when unanticipated, however, the models react differently. In general, the optimal response to a supply shock appears to be to do nothing. Increasing the money supply would always seem to be wrong; decreasing may be correct if the shock is permanent.

89　BLINDER, Alan S. and Stanley FISCHER (1981)
'Inventories, Rational Expectations, and the Business Cycle'
Journal of Monetary Economics, **8** (3), November: 277–304

The authors study mechanisms which create business cycles in the new classical economic school. They build two models of inventory holdings in which cycles are created by the adjustment of inventory stocks, but do not claim that inventories account for the entire postwar history of business cycles.

90 BLUME, L.E., M.M. BRAY and D. EASLEY (1982)
'Introduction to the Stability of Rational Expectations Equilibrium'
Journal of Economic Theory, **26** (2), April: 313–17

The authors survey the literature which examines the stability of agents' expectations in a RE equilibrium and discuss two frameworks. In the first, where there is convergence to a RE equilibrium, the agents must have extensive knowledge about the structure and dynamics of the prevailing model. The second framework yields an unstable RE equilibrium, but agents need not have correctly specified likelihood functions.

91 BLUME, Lawrence E. and David EASLEY (1984)
'Rational Expectations Equilibrium: An Alternative Approach'
Economic Theory, **34** (1), October: 116–29

The authors analyse a dynamic market in which traders condition their beliefs about parameters on past endogenously-generated market data and on current exogenous data. The market process is said to be informative if the beliefs of traders who receive only endogenously-generated market data approximate the true parameter value. They find RE equilibria can exist in the long run because the structure of the economy can be learned by Bayesians from endogenous market data.

92 BLUME, Lawrence E. and David EASLEY (1982)
'Learning to be Rational'
Journal of Economic Theory, **26** (2), April: 340–51

The authors examine the system of expectations generated by a simple general equilibrium model of an exchange economy in which each agent considers a finite collection of models which specify a relationship between payoff-relevant information and equilibrium prices. Can the traders accurately forecast information available to others by observing only the equilibrium price? If so, the forecast is a rational expectation. But nonrational expectations equilibria exist.

They find that in a Bayesian learning process the rational expectations equilibrium is locally stable, although nonrational equilibria may also be locally stable.

93   BOSCHEN, John F. and Herschel I. GROSSMAN (1982)
'Tests of Equilibrium Macroeconomics Using Contemporaneous Monetary Data'
Journal of Monetary Economics, (10): 309–33

The authors test the equilibrium approach of modelling the relation between monetary disturbances and macroeconomic fluctuations. The basic assumptions of these new classical models – market clearing and RE – imply that the known part of the monetary disturbance must be neutral. They find strong evidence against the validity of the equilibrium approach.

94   BRAY, Margaret (1985)
'Rational Expectations, Information and Assets Markets: An Introduction'
Oxford Economic Papers, **37** (2), June: 161–95

This is an introduction to the technically difficult literature on information in assets markets. Bray elaborates a standard deterministic partial equilibrium model of supply and demand in a spot market, with the added assumption that production decisions must be made before the market operates on the basis of price expectations. She then introduces a perfect foresight equilibrium – the deterministic rational expectations equilibrium. A futures market is introduced, as is the expected utility theory of choice under uncertainty.

95   BRAY, Margaret (1983)
'Convergence to Rational Expectations Equilibrium'
in Frydman and Phelps, 1980: 123–37

Bray discusses reasons for using the REH in light of recent work by herself and others on how agents learn to form RE. She concludes that the theory of the stability of RE equilibria needs to be improved.

96   BRAY, Margaret (1982)
'Learning, Estimation, and the Stability of Rational Expectations'
Journal of Economic Theory, **26** (2), April: 318–39

The stability of RE equilibrium in a simple asset market is studied
where a group of traders learn about the relationship between price
and return on an asset by using ordinary least squares estimation
and then those estimates to predict the return from the price. The
model estimated is a well-specified one of RE equilibrium, but
misspecified in terms of the situation in which the traders are learning. Bray finds that the model almost certainly converges to RE
equilibrium.

97   BRAY, M.M. and N.E. SAVIN (1986)
**'Rational Expectations Equilibria, Learning, and Model Specifica-
tion'**
Econometrica, **54** (5), September: 1129–60.

The authors analyse the stability of RE equilibrium for a version of
the cobweb model under learning. With conventional supply and
demand curves, the RE equilibrium is locally and globally stable.
When demand and supply curves take on an abnormal form, RE
equilibrium does not exist.

98   BROWN, Bryan and Schlomo MAITAL (1981)
**'What Do Economists Know? An Empirical Study of Experts' Expec-
tations'**
Econometrica, **49** (2), March: 491–504

The authors study the Livingston data to see whether they are
unbiased and whether complete use was made of all available information (the two conditions necessary for RE). They find little bias in
both half-year and full-year predictions, but discover extensive
underutilization of information.

99   BROZE, L., C. GOURIEROUX and A. SZAFARZ (1985)
'Solutions of Linear Rational Expectations Models'
Econometric Theory, **1**: 341–68

It is well known that linear RE models are problematic because of multiple solutions. The authors develop a global approach to treating all conceivable solutions which they determine by using a procedure based on revision processes.

100   BROZE, L. and A. SZAFARZ (1984)
'On Linear Models with Rational Expectations which Admit a Unique Solution'
European Economic Review, **24** (1), February: 103–11

The authors derive a reduced form of a RE linear model. Since their method is based on Dobb's theorem, no assumption on the structure of the stochastic process is required.

101   BRYANT, John (1983)
'Simple Rational Expectations Keynes–Type Model'
Quarterly Journal of Economics, **98** (3): 525–8

Bryant demonstrates that the RE position is not incompatible with Keynesian economics. He uses a 'Keynes-type model', incorporating assumptions of specialization and imperfect information.

102   BUCK, Andrew J. (1985)
'An Empirical Note on the Foundations of Rational Expectations'
Journal of Post Keynesian Economics, **7** (3), Spring: 311–23

Testing the weak form of RE, Buck finds that empirical evidence rejects the REH.

103   BUITER, Willem H. (1984)
'Saddlepoint Problems in Continuous Time Rational Expectations Models: A General Method and Some Macroeconomic Examples'
Econometrica, **52** (3), May: 665–80

Buiter presents the general solution method for RE models which can be represented by systems of deterministic first-order linear differential equations with constant coefficients. The method allows for numerical solutions of models with large numbers of state variables. Any combination of anticipated or unanticipated, current or future, and permanent or transitory shocks can be analysed.

104 BUITER, Willem H. (1983a)
'Expectations and Control Theory'
Economie appliquée, **36** (1): 129–56

For many years optimization techniques, which were originally developed for physical and engineering systems (such as dynamic programming and Hamiltonian methods), have been applied to social and especially to economic systems. But economists need to take into account at least two basic differences between physical and social systems. First, policy in social systems is not a game against nature, but a multiplayer game against rational agents. Secondly, the influence of expectations must be taken into account. Both the RE approach and the Lucas critique have posed a challenge to users of optimal control methods. Buiter analyses the problems and concludes that, with suitable modifications, these methods can remain useful to economists.

105 BUITER, Willem H. (1983b)
'Real Effects of Anticipated and Unanticipated Money – Some Problems of Estimation and Hypothesis Testing'
Journal of Monetary Economics, **11** (2): 207–24

Buiter builds on the work of Barro, showing other channels through which money can affect real variables. He also addresses estimation and testing of real effects of anticipated and unanticipated money.

106 BUITER, Willem H. (1981)
'The Superiority of Contingent Rules Over Fixed Rules in Models with Rational Expectations'
Economic Journal, **91** (363), September: 647–70

Buiter analyses the controversy between rules (without feedback or open loops) and discretion (flexible rules with feedback or closed-loop rules). He concludes that the RE revolution has weakened the case for conditionality in the design of policy rules (discretion).

107 BUITER, Willem H. (1980)
'The Macroeconomics of Dr. Pangloss: A Critical Survey of the New Classical Macroeconomics'
Economic Journal, **90** (357), March: 34–50

This is a survey article showing how the RE concept is a useful tool in economics. Optimal control theory should be used carefully in combination with RE. Buiter discusses the weaknesses of Lucas' 'surprise' supply function.

108   BULL, Clive and Roman FRYDMAN (1983)
'The Derivation and Interpretation of the Lucas Supply Function'
Journal of Money, Credit, and Banking, **15** (1), February: 82–95

The authors reformulate the Lucas and Rapping model to incorporate differences between local and global information. They derive the Lucas supply function from the Lucas-Rapping model of labour supply and then discuss problems relating to this genre of RE models.

109   BURMEISTER, Edwin (1980)
'On Some Conceptual Issues in Rational Expectations Modeling'
Journal of Money, Credit, and Banking, **12** (4), November, Part 2: 800–16

This is a discussion paper in which Burmeister concentrates on two issues: the problem of convergence of RE paths and the adjustment of prices.

110   BURMEISTER, Edwin, Robert P. FLOOD and Peter M. GARBER (1983)
'On the Equivalence of Solutions in Rational Expectations Models'
Journal of Economic Dynamics and Control, **5** (2/3), May: 311–21

This paper shows, first, that the 'forward-backward solution' to RE models is a special case of the 'market fundamentals plus bubble solution' and, second, that the 'spurious indicator solution' is equivalent to the 'market fundamentals plus bubble solution'. Thus instead of four types of solutions to RE macroeconomic models, there are actually only two.

111   BURMEISTER, Edwin and Stephen J. TURNOVSKY (1978)
'Price Expectations, Disequilibrium Adjustments, and Macroeconomic Price Stability'

Journal of Economic Theory, **17** (2), April: 287–311

The authors derive stability conditions for a model in which markets do not clear instantaneously, concluding that their assumptions are plausible but somewhat stringent. The novelty of their work consists in the parametrization of the degree of rationality of price expectations and the speed of market adjustment. Moreover they show that, given non-market-clearing conditions, RE in which actual and expected prices move in the same direction are consistent with stability.

112   BURTON, David (1983)
'Devaluation, Long-Term Contracts and Rational Expectations'
European Economic Review, **23** (1), September: 19–32

Burton considers the effects of devaluation and expected devaluation on output, prices and foreign exchange reserves in a small open economy with overlapping two-period wage contracts and RE. Devaluation has an expansionary effect on output if unanticipated when it occurs. Expected devaluations have no effect on prices until they take place. If devaluation is expected but does not occur, output falls. Reserves increase in response to all devaluations.

113   BUTLER, Alison and Christopher J. ELLIS (1988)
'Ranking Alternative Share Contracts under Rational Expectations'
European Economic Review, **32** (6), July: 1243–59

The authors compare share contracts to fixed and flexible nominal wages in a RE macromodel. They find that for nominal shocks, nominal movements are exacerbated by schemes which dampen real fluctuations. For real disturbances, a product wage reduces both real and nominal variability compared with other schemes. It also reduces employment when the marginal product of labour rises! If stability of the economy is desired, the authors find that the most effective action depends on the source of disturbance: a wage fund is desirable given supply disturbances, whereas a product wage is preferred given real disturbances.

114   CAGAN, Phillip (1980)
'Reflections on Rational Expectations'

Journal of Money, Credit, and Banking, **12** (4), November, Part 2: 826–32

As indicated in the title, the article is reflective: Cagan expresses his surprise that rational expectations were not developed earlier. He supports RE, but nonetheless discusses their limitations.

115   CALVO, Guillermo A. (1981)
'On the Time Consistency of Optimal Policy in a Monetary Economy'
in Lucas and Sargent, 1981: 639–58

This paper treats the time consistency of Ramsey-Friedman's optimal policy where such a policy maximizes a sum of instantaneous utilities which depend on consumption and monetary balances.

116   CALVO, Guillermo A. (1980)
'Tax-Financed Government Spending in a Neoclassical Model with Sticky Wages and Rational Expectations'
Journal of Economic and Dynamic Control, **2** (1), February: 61–78

Calvo analyses the impact of tax-financed government spending with constant nominal wages and RE and with no adjustment costs associated with capital accumulation. He finds that government policy can be an effective short-run policy tool in a world of perfect capital mobility and RE, so long as standard Keynesian assumptions are made regarding wage inflexibility and interest sensitivity to the demand for money.

117   CANTO, Victor A., Douglas H. JOINES and Robert I. WEBB (1984)
'Taxation, Rational Expectations, and the Neutrality of Money'
Journal of Macroeconomics, **6** (1), Winter: 69–78

The authors introduce progressive taxation of nominal income into a Barro-type monetary model with RE. Money is not neutral even in the long run. In the short run, unanticipated changes in the money supply cause output and prices to move in the same or opposite directions. They argue that these results are consistent with stagflation.

118   CARLSON, John A. (1977)
'A Study of Price Forecasts'

Annals of Economic and Social Measurement, **6** (1): 27–56

Carlson presents and analyses a data series on price expectations developed by Livingston (1947–75). He discusses problems in determining the rationality of the forecasts and emphasizes that economists should be extremely critical of expectations data.

119 CASS, David and Karl SHELL (1983)
'Do Sunspots Matter?'
Journal of Political Economy, **91** (2), April: 193–227

In this paper 'sunspots' refer to extrinsic uncertainty or random phenomena. The authors investigate whether or not RE equilibria are immune to influences from extrinsic uncertainty, or whether sunspots really matter. They find that they do. They also show that the traditional notion of equilibrium in dynamic models is too narrow.

120 CHAN, Kenneth S. (1982)
'Rational Expectations and the Optimal Foreign Exchange Regimes'
Canadian Journal of Economics, **15** (1), February: 164–74

Chan evaluates the optimality of fixed and flexible rates given RE and wage and price stickiness. The optimality of fixed or flexible rates depends on the efficiency and accuracy of the information received by agents. If current money supply or exchange rate is perfectly observable, the two exchange-rate regimes are identical despite wage and price stickiness.

121 CHENG, Hsueh-Cheng (1984)
'On the Generic Existence of Fully Revealing Price Equilibria'
Journal of Economic Theory, **32** (2), April: 351–8

Radner has established the generic existence of fully revealing RE equilibria, but in doing so he used an assumption which may not be true (one example being that the utility function is logarithmic). Cheng shows how a regularity condition can be imposed on the utility function to make Radner's assumption generically true.

122 CHERRY, Robert, Patrick CLAWSON and James W. DEAN (1981–82)
'Microfoundations of Macrorational Expectations Models'

Journal of Post Keynesian Economics, **4** (2), Winter: 214–30

The authors consider the new classical school's search for the micro-foundations of macroeconomics. RE models do not remove the requirement for asymmetric supply and demand behaviour of natural-rate hypothesis models. RE models require either the reten-tion of expectational, price-decision or informational asymmetries built into natural-rate hypothesis models or the introduction of a wealth effect on demand. They argue that these expectational asym-metries are inconsistent with the universal version of RE.

123   CHEVALLIER, François (1983)
      'Prévisions rationnelles: prévisions d'équilibre?' ('Rational Expec-tations: Equilibrium Expectations?')
      Economie appliquée, **36** (1): 47–73

The author argues that the relationship between RE and equilib-rium is in some ways simpler but in others more complex than RE advocates suggest. The discussion centres on uncertainty and RE.

124   CHOW, Gregory C. (1981a)
      'Estimation and Control of Rational Expectations Models'
      American Economic Review, **71** (2), May: 211–16

Chow shows how stochastic control techniques can be used to model economic behaviour and to estimate the parameters of RE models.

125   CHOW, Gregory C. (1981b)
      'Estimation and Optimal Control of Dynamic Game Models under Rational Expectations'
      in Lucas and Sargent, 1981: 681–9

Chow introduces two players and analyses the game on the assump-tion of a noncooperative Nash equilibrium. Treating government as the dominant player, he then considers policy evaluation by the government given RE.

126   CHOW, Gregory C. (1981c)
      'Estimation of Rational Expectations Models'

in Lucas and Sargent, 1981: 355–67

Chow analyses the estimation of linear rational expectations models when the objective function of the decision-maker is quadratic. He presents methods for maximum likelihood both in the general case and when the decision-maker's action is assumed to have no effect on the environment (the special case of perfect competition). He proposes a family of consistent estimators for the general case. In the final two sections he discusses problems with estimating linear RE models.

127 COLANDER, David C. and Robert S. GUTHRIE (1980–81)
'Great Expectations: What the Dickens Do "Rational Expectations" Mean?'
Journal of Post Keynesian Economics, **3** (2): 219–34

This is an introductory article on RE which is quite critical of the school. The authors conclude that RE is a mathematical tool for incorporating expectations into economic models. It is not a behavioural assumption; nor does it provide proof that people really behave rationally.

128 COOLEY, Thomas F. (1985)
'Individual Forecasting and Aggregate Outcomes: A Review Essay'
Journal of Monetary Economics, **15** (2), March: 255–66

Cooley reviews this collection edited by Roman Frydman and Edmund Phelps, arguing that they take too pessimistic a view of RE.

129 COUTINHO, Paulo C. (1986)
'Non-optimality of Rational Expectations Equilibrium: The Complete Markets Case'
Review of Economic Studies, **53** (5), October: 883–4

Coutinho shows that the conditions which guarantee uniqueness and optimality of Walrasian equilibrium under uncertainty are not sufficient to guarantee the same for a non-noisy RE equilibrium under asymmetric information.

130 CRAINE, Roger and Gikas A. HARDOUVELIS (1983)
'Are Rational Expectations for Real?'

Greek Economic Review, **5** (1), April: 5–32

This paper is also introductory in nature. The authors first focus on the theoretical issues involved in forming RE. In the second part they discuss practical considerations. Their tests for parameter stability indicate that the data do not form a basis for consensus RE.

131   CUDDINGTON, John T. (1982)
'Canadian Evidence on the Permanent Income-Rational Expectations Hypothesis'
Canadian Journal of Economics, **15** (2), May: 331–5

Repeating Hall's permanent-income RE tests using Canadian data, Cuddington finds that the empirical results are less favourable than those for the US. He notes that the empirical results for the UK published by Daly and Hadjimatheou in 1981 fully rejected the hypothesis.

132   CYERT, Richard M. and Morris H. DEGROOT (1974)
'Rational Expectations and Bayesian Analysis'
Journal of Political Economy, **82** (3), May–June: 521–36

The authors introduce the concept of Bayesian learning into models with RE and consistent expectations. Three different models are developed showing the interaction of Bayesian learning and expectations in achieving market equilibrium. The situation is such that the firm cannot immediately move to equilibrium.

133   DAGLI, C. Ates and John B. TAYLOR (1984)
'Estimation and Solution of Linear Rational Expectations Models Using a Polynomial Matrix Factorization'
Journal of Economic Dynamics and Control, **8** (3), December: 341–8

A relatively easy method to solve and estimate multivariate linear RE models is developed.

134   DAGUM, Camilo (1986)
'Analyzing Rational and Adaptive Expectations Hypotheses and Model Specifications'

Economies et sociétés, **20** (11), November: 15–34

Dagum discusses the 'poverty of RE' which he claims is ahistorical and does not stand up to empirical evidence. He defends Wold's model specifications – even with RE – for being more general than the adaptive and rational expectations models.

135 DANES, Michael (1975)
'The Measurement and Explanation of Inflationary Expectations in Australia'
Australian Economic Papers, **14** (24), June: 75–87

Danes constructs and examines a series of price expectations for Australia, briefly discussing their rationality. He outlines the problems and procedures, but indicates that the test is beyond the scope of his study.

136 DARRAT, Ali F. (1985)
'Anticipated Money and Real Output in Italy: Some Tests of a Rational Expectations Approach'
Journal of Post Keynesian Economics, **8** (1), Fall: 81–90

Darrat examines the empirical evidence for a RE natural-rate hypothesis for Italy. The results suggest that both anticipated and unanticipated money growth in Italy can induce positive deviations from trend in real output.

137 DAVIDSON, Paul (1982–83)
'Rational Expectations: A Fallacious Foundation for Studying Crucial Decision-Making Processes'
Journal of Post Keynesian Economics, **5** (2), Winter: 182–98

Davidson argues, first, that the REH is not a general theory of expectations formation and, second, that the REH analogy does not capture the crucial decision-making process of entrepreneurs. This is due to the nonergodicity of economic processes.

138 DAVIDSON, Paul (1981)
'A Critical Analysis of Monetarist-Rational Expectation-Supply Side (Incentive) Economics Approach to Accumulation during a Period of Inflationary Expectations'

Kredit und Kapital, **14** (4): 496–504

Davidson demonstrates that the monetarists' view that a sudden general increased (rational) expectation of inflation leads to a proportionate increase in the nominal interest rate, leaving the real interest rate unchanged, is incorrect. He argues that in this case the marginal efficiency of capital will rise.

139   DECANIO, Stephen J. (1979)
      'Rational Expectations and Learning from Experience'
      Quarterly Journal of Economics, **93** (1), February: 47–58

DeCanio is interested in how expectations evolve over time in a general setting. He develops a simple, plausible model of expectation modification in a market subject to random disturbances of a very general autocorrelated structure. He shows that convergence of expectations to RE depends on the nature of the learning process and on the structural and stochastic parameters of the market.

140   DEMERY, David (1984)
      'Aggregate Demand, Rational Expectations and Real Output: Some New Evidence for the U.K., 1963.2–1982.2'
      Economic Journal, **94** (376), December: 847–62

In his model Demery combines the Lucas-Sargent-Wallace (LSW) policy ineffectiveness proposition and the natural rate hypothesis-gradual adjustment of prices (NRH-GAP) hypothesis. The LSW proposition is rejected when the model is applied to UK data over the period from 1963.2 to 1982.2, when output surprises are allowed to influence nominal income growth, or when informational assumptions are less demanding. The data lend some support to the NRH-GAP model, although the assumptions allowing the model to hold are somewhat restrictive.

141   DICKINSON, D.G., M.J. DRISCOLL and J.L. FORD (1982)
      'Rational Expectations, Random Parameters and the Non-Neutrality of Money'
      Economica, **49** (195), August: 241–8

The authors prove that the Lucas-Sargent-Wallace policy ineffectiveness proposition is wrong. Since monetary policy can influence the variance of output, including its mean value, authorities should employ a money supply feedback rule.

142   DI TATA, Juan Carlos (1983)
'Expectations of Other's Expectations and the Transitional Nonneutrality of Fully Believed Systematic Monetary Policy'
with comment from C. Bull
in Frydman and Phelps, 1983: 47–68

Di Tata focuses on the money neutrality proposition of the new classical school. In his model he abandons some of the assumptions of the new classical models; for instance, his information assumption is less stringent. He finds that the short-run neutrality condition no longer holds. The results also suggest that Muth rationality may be achieved only in the long run.

143   DRISCOLL, M.J., J.L. FORD, A.W. MULLINEUX and S. SEN (1983a)
'Money, Output, Rational Expectations and Neutrality: Some Econometric Results for the U.K.'
Economica, **50** (199), August: 259–68

The authors report their empirical findings after testing UK data to see if the new classical neutrality of money proposition holds. They reject the view that monetary policy can have no effect on real output in the short run. They report their attempt to test the RE and structural neutrality (SN) hypotheses separately; both RE and SN restrictions are rejected.

144   DRISCOLL, M.J., J.L. FORD, A.W. MULLINEUX and S. SEN (1983b)
'Testing the Rational Expectations and Structural Neutrality Hypotheses'
Journal of Macroeconomics, **5** (3), Summer: 353–60

The authors develop a model of money growth and unemployment using the same data as Barro and Leiderman; contrary to that study, they find that the joint RE-structural neutrality hypothesis is rejected. They do, however, conjecture that small changes in the model may lead to different results. Thus they argue that little progress is likely to be made in judging the empirical relevance of RE until theoretical developments lead to a greater consensus about the true model of money growth and unemployment.

145   DRISCOLL, M.J., A.W. MULLINEUX and S. SEN (1985)
'**Testing the Rational Expectations and Structural Neutrality Hypothesis: Some Further Results from the U.K.'**
Empirical Economics, **10** (1): 51–8

Pointing out that most investigations of RE test both RE and structural neutrality (SN) assumptions together, the authors test both types of restrictions directly (that is, using the Lucas supply function and not an approximation). They find that the unrestricted model has a reasonably good fit, but when RE restrictions are imposed on it, they cannot be accepted. The authors warn that SN restrictions can only be tested by imposing them jointly on the model with RE restrictions.

146   DUBEY, Pradeep, John GEANAKOPOLOS and Martin SHUBIK (1987)
'**The Revelation of Information in Strategic Market Games: A Critique of Rational Expectations Equilibrium'**
Journal of Mathematical Economics, **16** (2): 105–37

The authors criticize the RE equilibrium approach to asymmetric information-general equilibrium because it does not explain how information is reflected in prices. They suggest instead a multiperiod game to explain the information process.

147   DUCK, N.W. (1983)
'**The Effects of Uncertainty about the Money Supply Process in a Rational Expectations Macroeconomics Model'**
Scottish Journal of Political Economy, **30** (2), June: 142–52

Duck uses a standard RE model to examine the implications for an uncertain money supply process. The uncertainty of this process consists in abrupt, partly unpredictable shifts in money supply. This added assumption may cause forecasts of monetary growth to produce errors which persist despite RE.

148   EICHENBAUM, Martin S. (1984)
**'Rational Expectations and the Smoothing Properties of Inventories
of Finished Goods'**
Journal of Monetary Economics, **14** (1), July: 71–96

In order to analyse the role of inventories the author uses a dynamic
RE equilibrium model in which production, inventories, sales and
prices are simultaneously determined.

149   EICHENBAUM, Martin (1983)
**'A Rational Expectations Equilibrium Model of Inventories of
Finished Goods and Employment'**
Journal of Monetary Economics, **12** (2), August: 259–77

The author constructs an equilibrium model of an industry which
produces and sells storable output. Assuming RE, he finds that the
equilibrium laws of motion of inventories and employment do not
'decompose' even under the assumption of perfect competition.

150   EVANS, George (1985)
**'Expectational Stability and the Multiple Equilibria Problem in
Linear Rational Expectations Models'**
Quarterly Journal of Economics, **100** (4), November: 1217–33

Linear models with expectations of future endogenous variables
often have multiple RE equilibria. Evans examines the stability of
solutions by investigating whether expectations return to a RE
equilibrium after having deviated from RE. He determines weak
and strong local stability.

151   EVANS, George (1983)
'The Stability of Rational Expectations in Macroeconomic Models',
with comment by G.A. Calvo
in Frydman and Phelps, 1983: 69–96

Evans shows that there are stability problems even if agents know
the true structure of the economy. He finds that RE equilibria
cannot be deduced from individual rationality alone, but require
collective consistency of expectations. He compares RE with Nash
equilibria.

152   EVANS, George W. and Riyaz GULAMANI (1984)
'Tests of Rationality in the Carlson-Parkin Inflation Expectations Data'
Oxford Bulletin of Economics and Statistics, **46** (1), February: 1–9

The authors test the UK inflation expectations series (1961–73) – the Carlson and Parkin series – for rationality to determine whether, given available information, it is unbiased. They find a deviation from full rationality.

153   EVANS, J.L. and G.K. YARROW (1979)
'Adaptive and Rational Expectations in Macroeconomic Models'
Manchester School of Economics and Social Studies, **47** (1), March: 24–32

It has been said that adaptive expectations become rational in the limit if people put no weight on past information. The authors prove this to be false.

154   FAIR, Ray C. (1979)
'An Analysis of a Macro-Econometric Model with Rational Expectations in the Bond and Stock Markets'
American Economic Review, **69** (4), September: 539–52

In this paper RE was first applied to a large-scale macro model – of the bond and stock markets. Fair finds that unanticipated policy actions are about 50 per cent as effective, and anticipated policy actions about 25 per cent as effective, when expectations are rational as opposed to when they are not.

155   FAIR, Ray C. (1978)
'A Criticism of One Class of Macroeconomic Models with Rational Expectations'
Journal of Money, Credit, and Banking, **10** (4), November: 411–17

Fair criticizes the extreme RE models of the new classical economists which postulate rationality with respect to expectations but not with respect to overall behaviour. When rationality of general behaviour is introduced into a RE model, the ineffectiveness of the anticipated policy result is reversed. Government can then influence real output by affecting the labour-leisure choice of households.

156 FAZZARI, Steven M. (1985)
'Keynes, Harrod, and the Rational Expectations Revolution'
Journal of Post Keynesian Economics, **8** (1), Fall: 66–80

Fazzari does not accept the new classical conclusion that the foundations of Keynesian economics have been refuted. He shows in a Keynes-Harrod framework that RE can lead to instability, strengthening the case for intervention in the market economy.

157 FEIGE, Edgar L. and Douglas K. PEARCE (1976)
'Economically Rational Expectations: Are Innovations in the Rate of Inflation Independent of Innovations in Measures of Monetary and Fiscal Policy?'
Journal of Political Economy, **84** (3): 499–522

The authors develop the concept of economically rational expectations to take account of the use and acquisition of information in forming expectations. RE avoid selecting an information set. Trying to reach a middle ground between adaptive and rational expectations, the authors find that adaptive expectation models may approximate an economically rational expectation formulation.

158 FELDMAN, Mark (1987)
'An Example of Convergence to Rational Expectations with Heterogeneous Beliefs'
International Economic Review, **28** (3), October: 635–50

Feldman discusses problems with the stability of RE equilibria in a model with Bayesian agents who initially possess a correct specification of the underlying structure of the economy but are uncertain about some parameters. Despite the heterogeneity of beliefs, there can be a convergence to RE equilibrium.

159 FELLNER, William (1980)
'The Valid Core of Rationality Hypotheses in the Theory of Expectations'
Journal of Money, Credit, and Banking, **12** (4), November, Part 2: 763–87

Fellner summarizes the background to the RE debate. He then

discusses the two central propositions of the strict version of RE, of which he is critical. In testing the REH he finds some support for it, warning, however, that regression analysis has limited value in deciding such complex issues.

160   FIELDS, T. Windsor and Nicholas R. NOBLE (1980)
'Rational Expectations and the Short-Run Phillips Curve: Comment'
Journal of Macroeconomics, **2** (2), Spring: 185–6

The authors criticize Lahiri and Lee's (1979) test of the REH which maintains that if the REH is true, the expected rate of inflation will be an unbiased predictor of the actual inflation rate. The authors argue that the Lahiri-Lee test is inadequate because the REH implies a much broader set of testable restrictions than lack of bias. Thus the Lahiri-Lee results are inconclusive.

161   FIGLEWSKI, Stephen and Paul WACHTEL (1981)
'The Formation of Inflationary Expectations'
Review of Economics and Statistics, **63** (1), February: 1–10

The authors use Livingston data to examine three expectations models. They find that inflation expectations in the postwar period were formed in a way inconsistent with the REH: as well as a downward bias there is evidence that individuals did not incorporate all the available information in their expectations. The adaptive expectations model best explains inflation expectations.

162   FISCHER, Stanley (1988)
'Recent Developments in Macroeconomics'
Economic Journal, **98** (391), June: 294–339

This survey includes sections on RE, the Phillips curve and business cycles.

163   FISCHER, Stanley (1980)
'On Activist Monetary Policy with Rational Expectations'
in Fischer, 1980: 211–47

Fischer accepts RE as a theory of expectations and endorses the view that unanticipated changes in the money supply have a greater effect on output than anticipated changes. He criticizes, however, the policy-ineffectiveness proposition of the new classical economists. Fischer argues that systematic countercyclical monetary policy can affect the behaviour of output and should be used to that end.

164   FISCHER, Stanley (1979)
      'Anticipations and the Nonneutrality of Money'
      Journal of Political Economy, **87** (2), April: 225–52

Fischer analyses the impact of anticipated and unanticipated changes in the money supply in a RE model in which money is not neutral. He explores phenomena other than the Phillips-curve type (Barro-Lucas) which cause nonneutralities of money.

165   FISCHER, Stanley (1977)
      'Long-Term Contracts, Rational Expectations, and the Optimal Money Supply Rule'
      Journal of Political Economy, **85** (1): 191–205
      rpt in Lucas and Sargent, 1981: 261–75

Fischer argues that activist monetary policy can affect the behaviour of real output even if expectations are rational. He offers a model with RE and overlapping contracts for two periods which inject wage-stickiness into the model. The money supply is changed more frequently than contracts and thus has the ability to affect the short-run behaviour of output.

166   FLOOD, Robert P. and Peter M. GARBER (1984)
      'Bubbles, Runs, and Gold Monetarization'
      in Paul Wachtel (ed.), *Crises in the Economic and Financial Structure*
      Lexington, Mass./Toronto: Lexington Books, 1984: 275–93

This paper focuses on price bubbles in RE models. The advent of the REH, with its emphasis on forward expectations, has revived the popularity of research on bubbles and runs. The authors construct a simple model to illustrate bubbles and runs and apply this to problems of gold monetarization.

167   FLOOD, Robert P. and Peter M. GARBER (1980)
'A Pitfall in Estimation of Models with Rational Expectations'
Journal of Monetary Economics, **6** (3), July: 433–5

The authors discuss a problem with an errors-in-variables RE model
which yields inconsistent parameter estimates.

168   FORMAN, Leonard (1980)
'Rational Expectations and the Real World'
Challenge, **23,** November–December: 36–9

Forman discusses the REH as embedded in new classical models, in
risk and uncertainty. He argues that the new classical models eliminate the uncertainty which characterizes economic phenomena.

169   FOURGEAUD, C., C. GOURIEROUX and J. PRADEL (1986)
'Learning Procedures and Convergence to Rationality'
Econometrica, **54** (4), July: 845–68

The authors use a macroeconomic model whose RE are the limits of
a learning process.

170   FOURGEAUD, Claude, Christian GOURIEROUX and Jacque-
line PRADEL (1984)
'Modèles à anticipations rationnelles: apprentissage par régression',
('Models with Rational Expectations: Learning by Regression')
Annales de l'INSEE, **54,** April–June: 63–77

This paper also deals with RE as a limit in a learning process. Using
regression on a linear model, they find a necessary and sufficient
condition for convergence to rationality.

171   FRATIANNI, Michele and Mustapha NABLI (1985)
'Inflation and Output with Rational Expectations in Open Economies'
Weltwirtschaftliches Archiv, **121** (1): 33–52

The authors develop a model of the real sector of a small, open
economy with RE which they test using yearly data from five EEC
member-countries from 1957 to 1980. They find that a large compo-

nent of the inflation rate was not anticipated. In four out of five countries the behaviour of output supports the hypothesis that internal and external relative prices play a significant role.

172 FRAZER, William J. Jr. (1978)
'Evolutionary Economics, Rational Expectations, and Monetary Policy', with comments from Steven Sheffrin and William K. Hutchison
Journal of Economic Issues, **12** (2), June: 343–404

Frazer investigates RE within the context of evolutionary economics.

173 FRIEDMAN, Benjamin M. (1980)
'Survey Evidence on the "Rationality" of Interest Rate Expectations'
Journal of Monetary Economics, **6** (4), October: 453–65

The author analyses predictions of six interest rates with time horizons of three to six months in advance over eight years. Friedman finds that the results were either mixed or did not support the REH. The tests show that survey respondents did not make unbiased predictions and that they did not always use information efficiently.

174 FRIEDMAN, Benjamin M. (1979)
'Optimal Expectations and the Extreme Information Assumptions of "Rational Expectations" Macromodels'
Journal of Monetary Economics, **5** (1), January: 23–41

Friedman examines the extreme assumptions of the REH, arguing that the crucial issue is to what extent the information availability assumption is valid. The information assumptions of the REH implicitly place models in a long-run context.

175 FRYDMAN, Roman (1983a)
'A Distinction Between the Unconditional Expectational Equilibrium and the Rational Expectations Equilibrium'
in Frydman and Phelps, 1983: 139–46

Frydman defines a notion of aggregate equilibrium called 'uncon-

ditional expectational equilibrium' where forecasts of the endoge-
neous variable are equal to the expected value of the probability
distribution of the variable. This equilibrium need not be optimal
because it is based on averages of individual expectations. This
result is considered to be an alternative to RE.

176   FRYDMAN, Roman (1983b)
      **'Individual Rationality, Decentralization, and the Rational Expec-
      tations Hypothesis'**
      in Frydman and Phelps, 1983: 97–122

Frydman reexamines the connections between the REH, the postulate of optimality of individual behaviour and the decentralization
of competitive markets. He finds that RE do not characterize expectations formation in decentralized markets.

177   FRYDMAN, Roman (1982)
      **'Towards an Understanding of Market Processes: Individual Expec-
      tations, Learning, and Convergence to Rational Expectations Equilib-
      rium'**
      American Economic Review, **72** (4), September: 652–68

In this paper Frydman shows the unlikelihood of convergence to
RE equilibrium in models of decentralized competitive markets in
which agents are assumed to be making individual decisions on the
basis of market prices and private information. He adds that the
analysis of market behaviour suggests that social norms may play a
significant role in understanding decentralized market processes.

178   FRYDMAN, Roman, Gerald P. O'DRISCOLL Jr. and Andrew
      SCHOTTER (1982)
      **'Rational Expectations of Government Policy: An Application of
      Newcomb's Problem'**
      Southern Economic Journal, **49** (2), October: 311–19

The authors discuss a particular problem with new classical RE
models: agents are required to know the model, but a number of
models may be relevant. This makes RE ambiguous. Building upon
Newcomb's problem, they argue that if a decision-maker must make
one of several decisions so that the payoff is affected by whether or

not his/her action is anticipated by an agent with good predictive powers, then a uniquely best rational course of action (or monetary policy) may not exist. They show that the REH is inconsistent.

179 **'Fur dumm verkaufen'** (1971)
     Der Spiegel, **49**, 29 November: 177ff.

This article considers recent developments of the new classical theorists, focusing on the policy inefficacy result. The author quotes Milton Friedman's belief that people can be systematically fooled for a considerably long time.

180 FUTIA, Carl A. (1981)
     'Rational Expectations in Stationary Linear Models'
     Econometrica, **49** (1), January: 171–92

Futia develops a method for analysing RE equilibria in linear economic models which enable one to determine whether or not the model has a RE equilibrium. If one exists, an explicit expression for the stochastic process of equilibrium prices can be found. His solution to finding an equilibrium – the method of z-transforms – does not impose such harsh restrictions on model assumptions as do former solutions.

181 GAHLEN, Bernard (1977)
     'Nur eine Ablenkung von der Problematik'
     Wirtschaftsdienst, **57** (2): 67–9

This is a short polemic against RE (no English summary).

182 GALEOTTI, Marzio (1984)
     'On the Micro-foundations of the Lucas Supply Function'
     Economic Notes, **13** (3): 115–27

The author shows how a Lucas supply function can be derived from a Lucas-Rapping microeconomic model cast in the RE island parable. He concludes that one must doubt the new classical policy ineffectiveness proposition.

183   GERTLER, Mark L. (1979)
'Money, Prices, and Inflation in Macroeconomic Models with Rational Inflationary Expectations'
Journal of Economic Theory, **21** (2), October: 222–34

Gertler concentrates on the problem of generating a unique solution in RE models. He concludes that some type of unsatisfactory restriction is necessary to generate determinate, stable price dynamics in RE macro models. Gertler shows how the assumption of imperfect price stability resolves the problem with the older approach of letting the price level jump to a stable path without explaining how this process to stability occurs.

184   GOMES, Gustavo Maia (1982)
'Irrationality of "Rational Expectations"'
Journal of Post Keynesian Economics, **5** (1), Fall: 51–65

Gomes argues that the neoclassical RE assumptions are too restrictive to be realistic and are thus irrational.

185   GOULD, John P. (1986)
'Is the Rational Expectations Hypothesis Enough?'
Journal of Business, **59** (4), October, Part 2: 371–7

Gould presents a RE model in which the REH does not restrict the number of equilibrium solutions in any meaningful way. He finds that the rationality assumptions often used in economic models may not significantly narrow the range of predicted economic behaviour.

186   GOURIEROUX, C., J.J. LAFFONT and A. MONFORT (1983)
'Révision adaptive des anticipations et covergence vers les anticipations rationnelles', ('Adaptive Revision of Expectations and Convergence to Rational Expectations')
Economie appliquée, **36** (1): 9–26

The authors determine under what conditions adaptive expectations converge to RE. They find that convergence can occur for a large range of adaptive mechanisms if the exogenous variables are not serially correlated and the RE model has a unique stationary solution.

187 GOWDY, John M. (1985–86)
'Rational Expectations and Predictability'
Journal of Post Keynesian Economics, **8** (2), Winter: 192–200

Gowdy argues that for RE models to be convincing the models must predict. He shows that the capacity of RE models correctly to predict is doubtful.

188 GRANGER, C.W.J. (1981)
'Investigating Causal Relations by Econometric Models and Cross-Spectral Methods'
in Lucas and Sargent, 1981: 371–86

Granger uses spectral methods to analyse causality and feedback problems in RE econometric models.

189 GREEN, Jerry R. and Seppo HONKAPOHJA (1983)
'Variance Minimizing Monetary Policies with Lagged Price Adjustment and Rational Expectations'
European Economic Review, **20** (1–3), January: 123–41

The authors examine a RE model in which prices are incompletely flexible so that markets do not clear. Monetary policy is not neutral. They find that the neutrality proposition is sensitive to the specification of the model, especially the price adjustment rule.

190 GREGORY, Allan W. and Michael R. VEALL (1985)
'A Lagrange Multiplier Test of the Restrictions for a Simple Rational Expectations Model'
Canadian Journal of Economics, **18** (1), February: 94–105

When RE econometric models are solved, they yield a set of testable nonlinear cross-equation restrictions. The authors develop a Lagrange multiplier test of such restrictions for a RE model.

191 GROSSMAN, Herschel I. (1983)
'The Natural-Rate Hypothesis, the Rational-Expectations Hypothesis, and the Remarkable Survival of Non-Market-Clearing Assumptions'

in *Variability in Employment, Prices, and Money,* Vol. 19 of the
Journal of Monetary Economics supplementary series
Amsterdam: North-Holland, 1983: 225–45

Grossman examines the merits of non-market-clearing models
which incorporate RE, compared to RE-market-clearing models
and market- and non-market-clearing models without RE. He finds
non-market-clearing models more realistic.

192   GROSSMAN, Herschel I. (1980)
'Rational Expectations, Business Cycles, and Government Behavior'
in Fischer, 1980: 5–22

This is the introduction to the conference on RE which was organized by Stanley Fischer in 1978. He reviews various issues relating to
business cycles, the NRH, the political process, RE, neutrality and
nonneutrality, and then summarizes the findings of the conference.

193   GROSSMAN, Jacob (1981)
**'The "Rationality" of Money Supply Expectations and the Short-Run
Response of Interest Rates to Monetary Surprises'**
Journal of Money, Credit, and Banking, **13** (4), November: 409–24

The author uses weekly survey data announced by the Fed to study
the rationality of money-supply expectations. He finds both that the
information is used efficiently and that expectations are revised. The
evidence supports the REH.

194   GROSSMAN, Sanford J. (1981)
**'An Introduction to the Theory of Rational Expectations under Asym-
metric Information'**
Review of Economic Studies, **48** (4), October: 541–59

Grossman outlines the evolution of the RE concept from a notion of
optimal forecasting to its virtual total departure from Walrasian
equilibrium.

195   GROSSMAN, Sanford J. (1977)
**'The Existence of Futures Markets, Noisy Rational Expectations and
Informational Externalities'**

Review of Economic Studies, **44**: 431–49

Grossman uses a RE model to analyse information and future markets. He finds that whenever profits are made by competitive firms learning inside information without existing futures markets, there will be a tendency for futures markets to develop.

196   GROSSMAN, Sanford J. (1975)
'Rational Expectations and the Econometric Modeling of Markets Subject to Uncertainty: A Bayesian Approach'
Journal of Econometrics, **3** (3), August: 255–72

Grossman shows that a RE price predictor is always unbiased and that RE equilibrium is a natural extension of competitive equilibrium.

197   GUISI, Luigi (1985)
'Crowding-out and Rational Expectations'
Giornale degli Economisti e Annali di Economia, **44** (5–6), May–June: 239–57

Most treatments of crowding out assume static expectations. Assuming that expectations are rational, Guisi finds that the slope of the LM curve is crucial for the stability of the system.

198   HABERLER, Gottfried (1980a)
'Critical Notes on Rational Expectations'
Journal of Money, Credit, and Banking, **12** (4), November, Part 2: 833–6

Haberler distinguishes between the 'hard-line' version of RE, which precludes efficacy of policy, and a more moderate monetarist position. The former he rejects; the latter he accepts.

199   HABERLER, Gottfried (1980b)
'Notes on Rational and Irrational Expectations', American Institute Reprint No. 11
rpt in Emil Küng (ed.), *Wandlungen in Wirtschaft und Gesellschaft: Die Wirtschafts-und die Sozialwissenschaften vor neuen Aufgaben* Tübingen: J.C.B. Mohr (Paul Siebeck), 1980

Here he argues that government actions cannot all be classified as systematic or unsystematic (as the new classical theory assumes); most fall between the two extremes. Haberler does not reject RE theory in a generalized form, but argues against the policy conclusions of the new classical economists. He does not believe the post-Keynesian consensus has been refuted by narrow versions of the REH, but rather enhanced by it.

200   HAHN, Frank (1983)
'Review of Begg's *The Rational Expectations Revolution in Macroeconomics*'
Economic Journal, **93**: 922–4

Hahn, clearly an opponent of the new classical RE models, writes a critical review of Begg's book (1982). He, nonetheless, acknowledges that the book serves as a useful textbook on RE.

201   HALL, Robert E. (1981)
'Stochastic Implications of the Life Cycle-Permanent Income Hypothesis: Theory and Evidence'
in Lucas and Sargent, 1981: 501–17

In this paper Hall models the marginal utility of consumption as a random walk in which the only variable of any value in predicting future consumption is current consumption. Tested for the US, the model is confirmed for real disposable income. Hall concludes that evidence exists for a RE version of the life cycle-permanent income hypothesis.

202   HALL, Robert E. (1980)
'"The Rational Expectations Approach to the Consumption Function: A Multi-Country Study" by Bilson: Comment'
European Economic Review, **13** (3), May: 301–303

Hall discusses Bilson's tests of the RE life cycle-permanent income hypothesis. He notes that although Bilson is very cautious, the evidence does not refute the hypothesis.

203   HALTIWANGER, John C. and Michael WALDMAN, (1985)
'Rational Expectations and the Limits of Rationality: An Analysis of Heterogeneity'

American Economic Review, **75** (3), June: 326–40

Since the problem of varying information among economic agents has largely been ignored, the authors construct two models in which the agents have different levels of information. The first group has RE and is referred to as 'sophisticated', whereas the second has incorrect expectations and is designated as 'naive'. The authors find three results. In a world of congestion effects, sophisticated agents have a disproportionately large effect on equilibrium; in a world characterized by synergistic effects, naive agents have a disproportionately large effect. In a repeating-game situation where reputation is important, either agent can dominate. The authors believe there is evidence to suggest that the economy may exhibit synergistic characteristics. More realistically, however, agents should be considered to possess heterogeneous abilities to gather and process information.

204 HAMILTON, James D. and Charles H. WHITEMAN (1985)
'The Observable Implications of Self-fulfilling Expectations'
Journal of Monetary Economics, **16** (3), November: 353–73

The authors find that by relaxing the dynamic specification of RE models, speculative bubbles (self-fulfilling, speculative price paths which characterize RE models) seem to vanish. The empirical evidence to support them disappears.

205 HAMMANN, Detlev (1979)
'Phillips-Kurve, rationale Erwartungen und die kontrakttheoretische Betrachtung des Arbeitsmarkts' ('The Phillips Curve, Rational Expectations and the Contract Theoretic Approach to Labor Markets')
Konjunkturpolitik, **25** (3): 156–79

Hammann provides a short survey of the development of Phillips curve theories including the formulation of the REH.

206 HANDA, Jagdish (1982)
'Rational Expectations: What Do They Mean?—Another View'
Journal of Post Keynesian Economics, **4** (4), Summer: 558–64

Handa discusses the differences between narrow and generalized RE.

207   HANSEN, Lars Peter and Thomas J. SARGENT (1982)
'Instrumental Variables Procedures for Estimating Linear Rational Expectations Models'
Journal of Monetary Models, **9** (3), May: 263–96

The authors show how to use instrumental variables procedures to estimate parameters of linear RE models.

208   HANSEN, Lars Peter and Thomas J. SARGENT (1981a)
'Exact Linear Rational Expectations Models: Specification and Estimation'
Research Department Staff Report 71, Federal Reserve Bank of Minneapolis, September 1981.

The authors describe how to specify and estimate for the small subclass of all possible RE models in which exact linear relationships exist between variables and expectations.

209   HANSEN, Lars Peter and Thomas J. SARGENT (1981b)
'Formulating and Estimating Continuous Time Rational Expectations Models'
Research Department Staff Report 75, Federal Reserve Bank of Minneapolis, October 1981.

The authors propose a method for estimating the parameters of continuous time stochastic RE models from discrete time observations. They propose a method to cope with the nonlinearities which arise in the cross-equation restrictions of RE models.

210   HANSEN, Lars Peter and Thomas J. SARGENT (1981c)
'Formulating and Estimating Dynamic Linear Rational Expectations Models'
in Lucas and Sargent, 1981: 91–125

The authors again consider methods of formulating and estimating dynamic linear RE econometric models. They derive a useful formula for cross-equation RE restrictions. Granger causality is also discussed.

211   HANSEN, Lars Peter and Thomas J. SARGENT (1981d)
'Rational Expectations Models for Dynamically Interrelated Variables'

in Lucas and Sargent, 1981: 127–56

The authors develop 'procedures for the rapid numerical computation and convenient mathematical representation of a class of multiple variable, linear stochastic rational expectations models' (p. 127). The paper is devoted to model formulation.

212   HANSEN, Lars P. and Thomas J. SARGENT (1980)
'Formulating and Estimating Dynamic Linear Rational Expectations Models'
Journal of Economic and Dynamic Control, **2** (1), February: 7–46

Hansen and Sargent describe procedures for dealing with dynamic, linear econometric RE models. They derive a formula for cross-equation RE restrictions. This paper is a response to the challenge of the Lucas critique.

213   HANSSON, Ingemar (1986)
'Market Adjustment and Investment Determination under Rational Expectations'
Economica, **53** (212), November: 505–14

The author analyses how a competitive market adjusts to an expected shift in demand in a RE model. Hansson concludes that capital adjustment is slow for an industry with long-lived capital, with an inelastic supply for investment goods and with a low elasticity of substitution between durable and nondurable inputs.

214   HARAF, William S. (1983)
'Tests of a Rational Expectations Structural Neutrality Model with Persistent Effects of Monetary Disturbances'
Journal of Monetary Economics, **11** (1), January: 103–16

The paper describes the results of tests of a RE structural neutrality model which consider the smoothing properties afforded to firms by holding stocks of inventories and back orders. The author aims to explain the persistence of real variables to unanticipated money growth as observed in the models of Barro and Rush; he finds that the models account for such persistence.

215   HEINER, Ronald A. (1985–86)
'Rational Expectations When Agents Imperfectly Use Information'

Journal of Post Keynesian Economics, **8** (2), Winter: 201–207

Heiner models both imperfect use of information (which is ignored by RE) and imperfect information. He finds that, contrary to popular opinion, RE do not imply optimal use of information. The imperfect use of information produces more systematic effects on behaviour than those resulting from imperfect information.

216   HELLWIG, Martin F. (1982a)
'Rational Expectations Equilibrium with Conditioning on Past Prices: A Mean-Variance Example'
Journal of Economic Theory, **26** (2), April: 279–312

The paper examines RE equilibrium in a dynamic model of the market in which agents condition their expectations on past rather than current market prices. Hellwig finds that markets can approximate informational efficiency even if the acquisition of information is costly.

217   HELLWIG, Martin F. (1982b)
'Rational Expectations and the Markov Property of Temporary Equilibrium Processes'
Journal of Mathematical Economics, **9** (1–2), January: 135–44

Hellwig discusses a sequence economy in which every sequence of selections of temporary equilibrium correspondences determines a Markov process. The unique RE equilibrium process is not of a Markov type.

218   HÉNIN, Pierre-Yves and André ZYLBERBERG (1983)
'Sur l'efficacité de la politique monétaire dans des modèles de prévisions rationnelles avec ajustement partiel des prix', ('On the Efficiency of Monetary Policy in Rational Expectations Models with Partial Price Adjustment')
Economie appliquée, **36** (1): 157–74

The authors aim to clarify the proposition that market clearing, and thus flexible prices, are not necessary conditions for the inefficacy of anticipated policy propositions. They consider alternative specifications of price adjustment rules and show that the Lucas-Sargent-Wallace policy inefficacy proposition does not hold.

219 HENRY, S.G.B. and S. WREN-LEWIS (1984)
'The Aggregate Labour Market in the United Kingdom: Some Experiments with Rational Expectations Models', with comments by Jean Waelbroeck
in Pierre Malgrange and Pierre-Alain Muet (eds.), *Contemporaneous Macroeconomic Modelling,*
Oxford: Basil Blackwell, 1984: 62–88

The authors use various models which incorporate the REH to analyse their ability to explain changes in employment. Few of them do so. They also find that, given expected output, RE models are less satisfactory than those based on cost minimization.

220 HILLIER, Brian (1985)
'Rational Expectations, the Government Budget Constraint, and the Optimal Money Supply'
Journal of Macroeconomics, **7** (1), Winter: 39–50

Hillier explores the new classical proposition that a purely deterministic money supply rule will have no effect on real output. Incorporating into this model the government budget constraint, which is a function of exogenous shocks to the system, he finds that a deterministic rule may not be valid.

221 HILLIER, Brian and James M. MALCOMSON (1984)
'Dynamic Inconsistency, Rational Expectations, and Optimal Government Policy'
Econometrica, **52** (6), November: 1437–51

This article focuses on 'dynamic inconsistency', that is, when a government's optimal policy changes over time – a problem first broached by Kydland and Prescott. Sheffrin (1983) found that when nondistorting taxes are used, optimal policies will remain consistent. The authors show that this does not hold for nonhomogeneous agents. They argue that inconsistency relates to the set of policy instruments which the government has at hand, not with lump-sum taxes.

222 HIRSCHHORN, Eric (1984)
'Rational Expectations and the Effects of Government Debt'

Journal of Monetary Economics, **14** (1), July: 55–70

Assuming incomplete information, Hirschhorn incorporates the effects of government debt into a RE model patterned after Barro. He extends the RE model to include the effects of debt issuance. Even when bonds do not constitute net wealth to the economy, he finds that bond issuance will appear expansionary; in other words, total debt outstanding and output are positively correlated.

223   HOEL, Michael (1979)
'Rational Expectations and Rigid Wages: A Model of Inflation and Unemployment'
Scandinavian Journal of Economics, **81** (3): 387–99

Hoel analyses wage rigidity in a RE model which implies that the short-run Phillips curve is not vertical, although the long-run curve is.

224   HOFFMAN, Dennis L. and Peter SCHMIDT (1981)
'Testing the Restrictions Implied by the Rational Expectations Hypothesis'
Journal of Econometrics, **15**: 265–87

The authors examine the nature and form of the restrictions imposed by the REH in various models. They find that such restrictions depend on the structure of the model and on the process generating exogenous variables.

225   HOLLAND, A. Steven (1985)
'Rational Expectations and the Effects of Monetary Policy: A Guide for the Uninitiated'
Federal Reserve Bank of St Louis Review, **67** (5), May: 5–11

Holland reviews the REH in the light of monetary theory. He discusses how models can be altered so that the new classical policy inefficacy result no longer holds; he also assesses the contribution of RE with respect to monetary policy.

226   HORNE, Jocelyn and Ian M. MCDONALD (1984)
'Rational Expectations, Gradual Price Adjustment and Monetary Policy in Australia'

Australian Economic Papers, **23** (42), June: 79–90

The authors examine a RE structural model which allows for gradual price adjustment. Using Australian data, they confirm that price adjustment is gradual – that is, prices do not adjust to clear markets within the quarter – causing the rejection of the RE-neutrality joint hypothesis. They conclude that the Australian economy. combines classical and Keynesian features.

227 **'How Expectations Defeat Economic Policy'** (1976)
Business Week, November 8: 74–5

This article describes the advent of new classical economics, emphasizing the policy inefficacy result.

228 HOWITT, Peter (1986)
'Conversations with Economists: A Review Essay'
Journal of Monetary Economics, **18** (1), July: 103–18

Howitt reviews Klamer's *Conversations with Economists* in which the latter interviews new classical economists and their opponents. Klamer argues that rhetoric or style of argument is the issue at the heart of new classical economics. Howitt disagrees.

229 HOWITT, Peter W. (1981)
'Activist Monetary Policy Under Rational Expectations'
Journal of Political Economy, **89** (2): 249–69

Howitt argues that activist monetary policy can be recommended even if people form expectations rationally. He constructs a simple model in which prices are costly to adjust, in which there is uncertainty about aggregate demand parameters, as well as positive costs involved in acquiring and using information.

230 HUNTZINGER, R. LaVar (1979)
'Market Analysis with Rational Expectations: Theory and Estimation'
Journal of Econometrics, **10** (2), June: 127–45

The author develops a solution to the fixed-point or equilibrium price sequence in a RE model. His approach reveals the relationship between exogenous structure, expectations and behaviour.

231   JAEGER, Klaus (1986)
'**Stabilisierungspolitik in kurzfristigen Einkommens- und Beschäfti-gungsmodellen mit rationalen Erwartungen**' ('**Stabilization Policy in Short-run Income and Employment Models with Rational Expectations**')
Jahrbücher für Nationalökonomie und Statistik, **201** (4), July: 329–49

Examining new classical RE and neoclassical models in relation to the policy inefficacy proposition, Jaeger finds that the effectiveness of policy depends not on fixed or flexible prices but on the form of the structural equations involved.

232   JAEGER, Klaus (1984)
'**Persistenz und zyklische Schwankungen der Unterbeschäftigung in Gleichgewichtsmodellen mit rationalen Erwartungen**' ('**Persistence and Cyclical Movements of Unemployment in Equilibrium Models with Rational Expectations**')
Zeitschrift für Wirtschafts- und Sozialwissenschaften, **104** (6): 645–73

By using four general equilibrium models with RE, Jaeger shows that cyclical movements in unemployment occur under two conditions: when there is a lagged labour supply function, or if the labour supply function is interdependently linked to other lagged quantity reaction functions so that individuals cannot separate permanent from transitory components of shocks. This latter problem causes persistence.

233   JOHNSON, Paul (1983)
'**Life-Cycle Consumption under Rational Expectations: Some Australian Evidence**'
Economic Record, **59** (167), December: 345–50

Johnson uses Australian data to test Hall's 1978 RE life cycle-permanent income consumption model. He finds the evidence for Australia more convincing than that relating to Canada or the UK.

234   JORDAN, J.S. (1985)
'**Learning Rational Expectations: The Finite Case**'

Journal of Economic Theory, **36** (2), August: 257–76

Jordan tackles the learning problem connected with RE models. He questions whether agents can learn RE from repeated observations of market data in a stationary environment with finitely many exogenous states of the world. Assuming that agents begin with no knowledge of their environment, he discovers an estimation procedure which does in fact converge to RE if the environment evinces a certain regularity.

235   JORDAN, J.S. (1982)
      'The Generic Existence of Rational Expectations Equilibrium in the Higher Dimensional Case'
      Journal of Economic Theory, **26** (2), April: 224–43

Focusing on the generic existence of RE equilibria, Jordan shows that when the dimension of the space of the states of private information is greater than the price space, there is a residual set of environments which permits equilibria which are arbitrarily close to fully revealing.

236   JORDAN, James S. and Roy RADNER (1982)
      'Rational Expectations in Microeconomic Models: An Overview'
      Journal of Economic Theory, **26** (2), April: 201–23

An introduction to research in general equilibrium theory of RE, this paper discusses the existence of exact and approximate RE equilibria, the implementation of equilibria, the behaviour of learning and smoothing processes by which agents construct expectations from repeated observations of the market, and the lagged use of information revealed by prices in an intertemporal sequence of markets. Jordan and Radner used this paper to introduce a *Journal of Economics* symposium on RE in microeconomic models.

237   JUNG, Woo S. (1986)
      'Optimal Stabilization Policies under Rational Expectations'
      Economic Modelling, **3** (2), April: 117–25

Jung investigates optimal stabilization policies when policy-makers have quadratic loss functions and when expectations are rational.

He finds solutions when future expectations are part of the model and also when they are not.

238   KANTOR, Brian (1979)
'Rational Expectations and Economic Thought'
Journal of Economic Literature, **17** (4), December: 1422–41

An introduction to RE, Kantor provides the reader with a brief history of RE and then discusses its significance within macro-economics. He concludes that the emphasis on expectations has had a positive effect on macroeconomics.

239   KARIYA, Takeaki (1983)
'Optimal Rational Expectations'
Hitotsubashi Journal of Economics, **24** (2), December: 101–108

Examining the REH, Kariya shows that expectation formation is not optimal relative to profit or sales maximization.

240   KATONA, George (1980)
'How Expectations Are Really Formed'
Challenge, **23**, November–December: 32–5

Katona objects to RE, arguing that economists should consider psychological evidence about expectations formation. He argues that empirical research (surveys) can be used to determine what expectations are and how they have changed.

241   KAUFMAN, Roger T. and Geoffrey WOGLOM (1983)
'Estimating Models with Rational Expectations'
Journal of Money, Credit, and Banking, **15** (3), August: 275–85

Focusing on estimation problems with RE models and starting with the Lucas critique, the authors argue that procedures which include structural stability among their hypotheses are not promising. They propose procedures which do not incorporate a stationary assumption.

242   KAWAI, Masahiro (1983)
'Price Volatility of Storable Commodities under Rational Expectations in Spot and Futures Markets'

International Economic Review, **24** (2), June: 435–59

Kawai studies the effect of commodity futures on the process of price formation under RE. He finds that a futures market may extend the scope of successful price stabilization through government intervention.

243 KENNAN, John (1979)
'The Estimation of Partial Adjustment Models with Rational Expectations'
Econometrica, **47** (6), November: 1441–55

The author analyses the implications for RE embedded in a partial-adjustment model and finds the results encouraging.

244 KIMBROUGH, Kent P. (1984)
'The Derivation and Interpretation of the Lucas Supply Function: A Comment'
Journal of Money, Credit, and Banking, **16** (3), August: 367–77

Kimbrough comments on Bull and Frydman's paper (1983) in which they argue that the Lucas supply function cannot be derived as a structural equation from the Lucas-Rapping framework as is claimed. The author shows that Bull and Frydman's result stems from a misinterpretation of Lucas' island parable.

245 KING, Robert G. (1981)
'Monetary Information and Monetary Neutrality'
Journal of Monetary Economics, **7** (2): 195–206

King modifies those Lucas-Barro-Sargent equilibrium business cycle models which assume that monetary aggregates are not directly observable during the period under study, generating monetary nonneutrality based on misperceptions of the price level. Assuming instead that money is accurately observable, King finds that real activity does not correlate with monetary data.

246 KIRMAN, Alan (1983)
'On Mistaken Beliefs and Resultant Equilibria' with comment from J. Green

in Frydman and Phelps, 1983: 147–68

Kirman constructs a simple RE model to show that a reasonable learning process will not necessarily overcome the problem of mis-specification. Improving the learning process or the model does not change this result. He also finds that a whole class of outcomes in his model may be a final equilibrium, the one actually observed being determined by arbitrary initial conditions. To conclude, the characterization of possible equilibria may be of greater significance than stability.

247   KLAMER, Arjo (1983)
'Empirical Arguments in New Classical Economics'
Economie appliquée, **36** (1): 229–54

Focusing on the empirical research of the new classical economists, Klamer suggests that the main novelty of the new classical school lies in the style of its argumentation.

248   KÖNIG, H. (1980)
'"The Rational Expectations Approach to the Consumption Function: A Multi-Country Study" by Bilson: Comment'
European Economic Review, **13** (3), May: 305–308

König comments on Bilson's paper, outlining some problems with his econometric model, its drawbacks, and the restrictiveness of its assumptions.

249   KUGLER, Peter (1982)
'Konsum, Einkommen und rationale Erwartungen: empirische Ergebnisse für die Schweiz' ('Consumption, Income and Rational Expectations: Some Empirical Results for Switzerland')
Kyklos, **35** (3): 500–15

Kugler tests the RE version of the life cycle hypothesis of consumption for Switzerland. The hypothesis (with a neo-Ricardian definition of disposable income) was rejected and the test as usually defined brought no significant results. The findings raise doubts about the specification of the consumption function.

250 KYDLAND, Finn and Edward C. PRESCOTT (1980)
'A Competitive Theory of Fluctuations and the Feasibility and Desirability of Stabilization Policy' with comments by Feldstein and Taylor
in Fischer, 1980: 169–98

The authors find that tax rates do not respond to aggregate economic fluctuations. Using a RE equilibrium business cycle model, they find that the economy can be stabilized, but that the costs are greater than the benefits. This is an attempt to link the theory of modern finance with that of macroeconomics.

251 KYDLAND, Finn E. and Edward C. PRESCOTT (1977)
'Rules Rather than Discretion: The Inconsistency of Optimal Plans'
Journal of Political Economy, **85** (3), June: 473–91
rpt in Lucas and Sargent, 1981: 619–37

In this important paper, the authors find that 'if there is an agreed upon, fixed social objective function and policy makers know the timing and magnitude of the effects of their actions, discretionary policy, namely, the selection of that decision which is best, given the current situation and a correct evaluation of the end-of-period position, does not result in the social objective function being maximized. The reason for this apparent paradox is that economic planning is not a game against nature but, rather, a game against rational economic agents.' They conclude that, given RE, there is no way that control theory can successfully be applied to economic planning.

252 LAD, F. (1983)
'A Subjectivist View of the Rational Expectations Hypothesis: Critique and Development'
Metroeconomica, **35**: 29–51

Reformulating the REH in terms of subjectivist probability, Lad shows how the identification of expanded expectations distributions can yield useful information.

253 LAFFONT, Jean-Jacques M. (1985)
'On the Welfare Analysis of Rational Expectations Equilibria with Asymmetric Information'

Econometrica, **53** (1), January: 1–29

This paper belongs to the microeconomic RE literature. RE equilibria are analysed as incentive-compatible mechanisms, and a welfare analysis made. The fully revealing RE equilibrium is found to be *ex-post* Pareto optimal.

254   LAHIRI, Kajal (1980)
'Rational Expectations and the Short-Run Phillips Curve: Reply and Further Results'
Journal of Macroeconomics, **2** (2), Spring: 187–92

The authors agree with Fields and Noble that their test may be inadequate because it fails to investigate a broader set of testable restrictions implied by the REH. They show that the restrictions implied by the REH in their wage-price model are consistent with available data at a reasonable level of statistical confidence.

255   LAHIRI, Kajal and Jung Soo LEE (1979a)
'Rational Expectations and the Short-Run Phillips Curve'
Journal of Macroeconomics, **1** (2), Spring: 167–90

The authors test the REH in the context of a wage-price model of the US economy. The empirical evidence shows that a short-run Phillips curve is nonexistent; also that the public expectations of inflation are actually conditional mathematical expectations based on all available information.

256   LAHIRI, Kajal and Jung Soo LEE (1979b)
'Tests of Rational Expectations and Fisher Effect'
Southern Economic Journal, **46** (2), October: 413–24

The authors test the REH and the Fisher effect as two distinct propositions. Their findings provide additional econometric evidence on the efficiency of the six-month treasury bill market. The REH implied a Fisher coefficient of only about 0.54. They find the observed rate of inflation does not seem to be an unbiased proxy for unobservable price expectations.

257   LAHIRI, Kajal and Y.H. LEE (1981)
'An Empirical Study on the Econometric Implications of Rational Expectations Hypothesis'

Empirical Economics, **6** (2): 111–27

The authors test the REH and find evidence both for it and for the NRH.

258   LANG, Harald (1985)
'Expectations and the Neutrality of Money: A Comment'
Journal of Economic Theory, **36** (2), August: 392–3

Commenting on Lucas' articles of 1972 and 1983, Lang points out that the flaw in the former can easily be corrected.

259   LAWRENCE, Colin (1983)
'Rational Expectations, Supply Shocks and the Stability of the Inflation-Output Tradeoff: Some Time Series Evidence for the United Kingdom, 1957–1977'
Journal of Monetary Economics, **11** (2): 225–45

The author modifies the Lucas supply curve (1973) to incorporate specific and aggregate supply and demand shocks. He develops a time series test of the REH–NRH. Using data for the UK, he finds that a significant reduction in the short-run inflation-output trade-off is associated with an increase in the variance of the unanticipated price level – evidence in favour of the REH–NRH. The higher variance was not attributed to demand but to supply shocks.

260   LAWSON, Tony (1981)
'Keynesian Model Building and the Rational Expectations Critique'
Cambridge Journal of Economics, **5** (4), December: 311–26

Lawson condemns the new classical criticisms of Keynesian model building, arguing that they are inaccurate in labelling certain views as Keynesian. Many of the points made by the new classicists are well understood and accepted by Keynesians.

261   LEE, Susan (1984)
'The Un-Managed Economy'
Forbes, December: 147–58

This is a very readable introduction to RE for nonspecialists which includes a discussion of the historical background from which RE emerged.

262   LEIDERMAN, Leonardo (1980)
'Macroeconometric Testing of the Rational Expectations and Structural Neutrality Hypotheses for the United States'
Journal of Monetary Economics, **6** (1), January: 69–82

Leiderman's paper is concerned with the joint testing of the RE and structural neutrality hypotheses. He also devises a method to test them separately. US data do not reject either structural neutrality or the REH.

263   LEIDERMAN, Leonardo (1979)
'Expectations and Output-Inflation Tradeoffs in a Fixed-Exchange Rate Economy'
Journal of Political Economy, **87** (6), December: 1285–1306

Leiderman develops a reverse Phillips curve model of output-inflation tradeoffs for a fixed-exchange economy, incorporating the REH and several forms of the NRH. The model is tested using data for Italy (1955–70). The REH was not rejected, nor was the joint REH–NRH in conflict with the sample information. These results seem to support new classical assumptions.

264   LEIJONHUFVUD, Axel (1983a)
'Keynesianism, Monetarism, and Rational Expectations: Some Reflections and Conjectures' with comment by Hahn
in Frydman and Phelps, 1983: 203–30

In this paper Leijonhufvud reflects on problems with Keynesian economics, the new classicism and monetarism.

265   LEIJONHUFVUD, Axel (1983b)
'What Would Keynes Have Thought of Rational Expectations?'
in David Worswick and James Trevitheck (eds.), *Keynes and the Modern World: Proceedings of the Keynes Centenary Conference, King's College, Cambridge*
Cambridge: Cambridge University Press, 1983: 179–205

In another very readable article, Leijonhufvud attempts to put new classicism, Keynes, Keynesians, monetarism and RE into perspective. This article is well worth reading.

266 LEONARD, Jonathan S. (1982)
'Wage Expectations in the Labor Market: Survey/Evidence on Rationality'
Review of Economics and Statistics, **64** (1), February: 157–61

Leonard argues that the assumption of RE is unfounded. He observes price expectations of executives who are in the market every year and should, thus, learn from experience. He finds that their wage expectations are not rational and therefore concludes that RE do not characterize market expectations.

267 LEVINE, Paul (1986)
'The Formulation of Robust Policies for Rival Rational Expectations Models of the Economy'
Journal of Economic Dynamics and Control, **10** (1/2), June: 93–7

Levine concentrates on the problem which arises when some models assume RE. He develops a general method for deriving policies which are robust with respect to several different RE models of the economy.

268 LIPTON, David, James POTERBA, Jeffery SACHS and Lawrence SUMMERS (1982)
'Multiple Shooting in Rational Expectations Models'
Econometrica, **50** (5), September: 1329–33

The authors address problems of finding solutions to nonlinear RE models. The approach, called 'multiple shooting', is taken from engineering.

269 LISSNER, Will (1985)
'A New School of Economic Theorists: The "New Classical Economists"'
American Journal of Economics and Sociology, **44** (2), April: 255–6

This is a short review of Klamer's *Conversations with Economists.*

270   LITTERMAN, Robert B. and Laurence WEISS (1985)
'Money, Real Interest Rates, and Output: A Reinterpretation of Post-war U.S. Data'
Econometrica, **53** (1), January: 129–56

The authors re-examine time-series evidence that changes in the money supply have been an important factor in generating postwar business cycles. They find their 'dynamic IS-LM' model with RE to be compatible with observed movements between money, interest rates, inflation and output.

271   LONG, John B. and Charles I. PLOSSER (1983)
'Real Business Cycles'
Journal of Political Economy, **91** (1), February: 39–69

The authors show how normal economic principles lead maximizing individuals to choose consumption-production plans which display business cycle behaviour. Their explanation is consistent with the REH.

272   LOVELL, Michael C. (1986)
'Tests of the Rational Expectations Hypothesis'
American Economic Review, **76** (1), March: 110–24

This paper reviews the evidence from various empirical studies challenging the validity of the REH. Lovell finds that cumulative empirical evidence does not establish its superiority over alternative hypotheses. He reviews various methods of modelling expectations and then discusses the evidence, concluding that 'the weight of empirical evidence is sufficiently strong to compel us to suspend belief in the hypothesis of RE, pending accumulation of additional evidence' (p. 122). He prudently suggests that there should be more testing of the REH against its alternatives. This paper is recommended reading for all economists.

273   LOWENBERG, A.D. (1982)
'A Critical Assessment of the Macro Rational Expectations Paradigm'
South African Journal of Economics, **5** (3), September: 208–24

Lowenberg investigates the theoretical underpinnings of classical

REH and Keynesian models. He concludes that both groups make *ad hoc* assumptions and that the new classical economists and Keynesians generally emphasize different transaction costs. This article is highly recommended.

274 LUCAS, Robert E. (1986)
'Adaptive Behavior and Economic Theory'
Journal of Business, **59** (4), October, Part 2: 401–26

Here Lucas uses cases to illustrate adaptation and rationality in economic theory. He argues that adaptation and rationality are complementary and that stability theories based on adaptive behaviour can help to narrow the set of empirically interesting equilibria in economic models.

275 LUCAS, Robert E. (1983)
'Expectations and the Neutrality of Money'
Journal of Economic Theory, **31** (1), October: 197–9

Here Lucas tries to correct for the logical error in his 1972 paper, as identified by Grandmont.

276 LUCAS, Robert E. (1981a)
'Capacity, Overtime, and Empirical Production Functions'
in Lucas, 1981: 146–55
rpt in *American Economic Review: Papers and Proceedings,* **60**, 1970: 23–7

Lucas examines two margins along which a firm may increase its labour-capital ratio. He then offers an alternative model with an empirical production function.

277 LUCAS, Robert E. (1981b)
'Distributed Lags and Optimal Investment Policy'
in Lucas and Sargent, 1981: 39–54

This paper is an examination of optimal investment policy. Lucas attempts to determine a firm's optimal investment plan in the presence of gestation lags and under various assumptions about depreciation.

278   LUCAS, Robert E. (1981c)
'Econometric Testing of the Natural Rate Hypothesis'
in Lucas, 1981: 90–103
rpt in Otto Eckstein (ed.), *The Econometrics of Price Determination Conference,*
Washington, D.C.: Board of Governors of the Federal Reserve System, 1972: 50–9

In this well-known paper Lucas tries to capture the natural rate hypothesis in a testable model. He finds, first, that the adaptive expectations hypothesis does not lead to a hypothesis of a natural rate of output. The two are contrary and thus econometric models using adaptive expectations cannot test the NRH. Second, the REH does lead to a natural rate theory. Third, the NRH does not imply a Phillips curve but is consistent with quantitative policy evaluation.

279   LUCAS, Robert E. (1981d)
'An Equilibrium Model of the Business Cycle'
in Lucas, 1981: 179–214
rpt in the *Journal of Political Economy,* **83**, December 1975: 1113–44

In this famous paper Lucas develops an equilibrium model of the business cycle: prices and quantities are determined in competitive equilibrium; expectations are rational; information is imperfect. Business cycles are generated by unanticipated monetary-fiscal shocks.

280   LUCAS, Robert E. (1981e)
'Optimal Investment with Rational Expectations'
in Lucas and Sargent, 1981: 55–66

Using a RE model Lucas shows that the equations governing the behaviour of firms in competitive industry through time can be regarded as necessary conditions for the maximization of 'discounted consumer surplus'.

281   LUCAS, Robert E. (1981f)
'Real Wages, Employment, and Inflation'
in Lucas, 1981: 19–58
rpt from the *Journal of Political Economy,* **77**, September–October 1969: 721–54

Lucas constructs a model of the labour market which reconciles current divergent views on labour supply. He then tests the model on US time series (1929–65).

282   LUCAS, Robert E. (1981g)
'A Review: Paul McCracken *et al. Towards Full Employment and Price Stability*, A Report to the OECD by a Group of Independent Experts OECD, June 1977'
in Lucas, 1981: 262–70
rpt from *Policies for Employment, Prices, and Exchange Rates,* Vol. 11 of the supplement to Karl Brunner and Allan Meltzer (eds.), *Journal of Monetary Economics,*
Amsterdam: North-Holland, 1976: 161–8.

In this review Lucas attacks Keynesian activist macroeconomic theory. The problems with orthodox theory delineated here provided the stimulus for the development of the new classical theory.

283   LUCAS, Robert E. (1981h)
'Unemployment in the Great Depression: Is There a Full Explanation?'
in Lucas, 1981: 59–65
rpt in the *Journal of Political Economy,* **80**, January–February 1972: 186–91

Here Lucas replies to Reese's comment regarding the Lucas-Rapping paper of 1970.

284   LUCAS, Robert E. (1981i)
'Unemployment Policy'
in Lucas, 1981: 240–7
rpt in the *American Economic Review: Papers and Proceedings,* **68** (2), May 1978: 353–7

Lucas argues for the new classical view that unemployment is due to distortions from taxes, external effects, etc.

285   LUCAS, Robert E. Jr (1980a)
'Methods and Problems in Business Cycle Theory'

Journal of Money, Credit, and Banking, **12** (4), November, Part 2: 696–715
rpt in Lucas, 1981: 271–96

In this paper Lucas reviews historically recurring problems of business cycle theory within the framework of the neoclassical synthesis and within general equilibrium theory. He concludes by discussing future directions.

286   LUCAS, Robert E. (1980b)
'Rules, Discretion, and the Role of the Economic Advisor'
in Fischer, 1980: 199–210
rpt in Lucas, 1981: 248–61

In this famous paper Lucas defends Friedman's policy conclusions favouring a fixed policy rule.

287   Lucas, Robert E. Jr (1977)
'Understanding Business Cycles'
in Karl Brunner and Allan Meltzer (eds.), *Stabilization of the Domestic and International Economy*, Vol. 5 of the *Journal of Monetary Economics* supplementary series
Amsterdam: North-Holland, 1977, 7–29
rpt in Lucas, 1981: 215–39

Here Lucas again discusses the new classical approach to business cycles.

288   LUCAS, Robert E. Jr (1976)
'Econometric Policy Evaluation: A Critique'
in Karl Brunner and Allan H. Meltzer (eds.), *The Phillips Curve and Labor Markets,* Vol. 1 of the *Journal of Monetary Economics* supplement series, the *Carnegie-Rochester Conference Series on Public Policy,*
Amsterdam: North-Holland, 1976, 19–46
rpt in Lucas, 1981: 104–30

In this article Lucas develops his well-known 'Lucas critique': changes in policy will systematically alter the structure of econometric models.

289 LUCAS, Robert (1973)
'Some International Evidence on Output-Inflation Tradeoffs'
American Economic Review, **63** (3), June 1973: 326–34
rpt in Lucas, 1981: 131–45

Lucas tests the real output-inflation tradeoffs for 18 countries (1951–67). He finds that the higher the variance of demand, the more unfavourable are the terms of the Phillips curve tradeoff. In the 1981 reprint an 'Errata' appears, giving details of mistakes in the paper.

290 LUCAS, Robert E. (1972)
'Expectations and the Neutrality of Money'
Journal of Economic Theory, **4** (2), April: 103–24
rpt in Lucas, 1981: 66–89

A Phillips curve relationship is derived without the presence of money illusion. (Money is a veil.) Prices are market-clearing; agents behave optimally; expectations are rational (i.e. optimal). Because information is inadequate to permit agents to distinguish real from monetary disturbances, monetary fluctuations lead to real output movements in the same direction. In this model the Phillips curve is a central feature of the solution to a general equilibrium system.

291 LUCAS, Robert E. and Edward PRESCOTT (1981)
'Equilibrium Search and Unemployment'
in Lucas, 1981: 156–78
rpt in the *Journal of Economic Theory,* **7** (2), February 1974: 188–209

Lucas focuses on the question of why people choose to be unemployed rather than work at a low wage rate. He develops a model in which stochastic processes determine the solution.

292 LUCAS, Robert E. and Edward C. PRESCOTT (1971)
'Investment Under Uncertainty'
in Lucas and Sargent, 1981: 67–90
rpt in *Econometrica,* **39** (5), September 1971: 659–81

The authors extend the cost-of-adjustment type investment theory to situations involving demand uncertainty. Using an equilibrium model and assuming optimizing behaviour, they introduce the narrow version of RE.

293 LUCAS, Robert E. and L.A. RAPPING (1969)
'Real Wages, Employment and Inflation'
Journal of Political Economy, **77** (5): 721–54

In this paper Lucas and Rapping first derive the famous Lucas aggregate supply function from a two-period consumer decision model in which consumers must choose between current and future consumption of goods and leisure.

294 LUCAS, Robert E. and Thomas J. SARGENT (1978)
'After Keynesian Macroeconomics'
in *After the Phillips Curve: Persistence of High Inflation and High Unemployment,* The Federal Reserve Bank of Boston Conference Series No. 19
Boston: Federal Reserve Bank of Boston, 1978, 49–72, with 'Discussion' by B. Friedman (73–80), 'Response to Friedman' (81–2) and 'Rebuttal' (83)
rpt without discussion in Lucas and Sargent, 1981: 295–319

In this well-known article Lucas and Sargent discuss the failures of Keynesian macroeconomics and the advantages of equilibrium business cycle theory.

295 MACHLUP, Fritz (1983)
'The Rationality of "Rational Expectations"'
Kredit und Kapital, **16** (2): 172–83

In this last article written by Machlup before his death, he argues against the narrow version of the REH because it is irrational.

296 MADDOCK, Rodney (1984)
'Rational Expectations: A Lakatosian Case Study in Program Adjustment'
History of Political Economy, **16** (2), Summer: 291–309

In this paper Maddock uses the Lakatosian philosophy of science to analyse new classical economists. He finds that their programme is still 'immature'.

297 MADDOCK, Rodney and Michael CARTER (1982)
'A Child's Guide to Rational Expectations'
Journal of Economic Literature, **20** (1), March: 39–51

This is an entertaining introduction to RE. The authors conclude that the 'fundamental simplicity of the ideas involved has become obscured by overly rigorous development, and especially by the unconvincing resort to extraneous constructions, such as the "islands" mentioned above' (p. 49).

298 MAKINEN, Gail E. (1983)
'Recent Developments in Macroeconomic Theory and Policy'
Atlantic Economic Journal, **11** (4), December: 84–88

Makinen discusses new classical economics as part of a larger survey of modern economics, also examining the work of Barro. Makinen concludes that the major influence of the school has been to question the usefulness of model simulations, to revise how economists model expectations, and to emphasize that economic agents build anticipations of government policy into expectations (thus possibly reducing the effectiveness of government measures).

299 MANKIW, N. Gregory (1988)
'Recent Developments in Macroeconomics: A Very Quick Refresher Course' with comments by Herbert Stein, and Edmund Phelps
Journal of Money, Credit, and Banking, **20** (3), August, Part 2: 436–58

This is another survey of macroeconomic developments which includes RE. Mankiw concludes that the notion of (generalized) RE is 'no longer controversial among macroeconomists' (p. 447).

300 MARION, Nancy Peregrim (1982)
'The Exchange-Rate Effects of Real Disturbances with Rational Expectations and Variable Terms of Trade'
Canadian Journal of Economics, **15** (1), February: 104–18

Marion uses a stochastic macroeconomic model with RE and variable terms of trade to examine the initial exchange-rate response to fiscal policy and other real disturbances which may be anticipated or unanticipated, temporary or permanent, domestic or foreign.

301   MASHIYAMA, Koichi (1983)
'An Inventory Stock Market in a Business Cycle Model and Rational Expectations'
Economic Studies Quarterly, **34** (3), December: 211–24

Presenting a stock-oriented business cycle model with RE, the author examines how the inclusion of the inventory market alters the response of prices and interest rates. He finds that active speculation in the commodity stock market stabilizes price movements.

302   MAUSSNER, Alfred (1985)
'Ineffektivität der Wirtschaftspolitik bei "rationalen Erwartungen"? Ein Kommentar mit anderen Argumenten für eine unzureichend begründete These' ('Ineffectiveness of Economic Policy under "Rational Expectations"? A Commentary Offering Other Arguments for an Insufficiently Founded Thesis')
Kredit und Kapital, **18** (2): 217–29

Maussner rejects the new classical policy ineffectiveness proposition, but not on the same grounds as those put forward by Ramb. He 'corrects' Ramb's argument.

303   MAYES, David G. (1981)
'The Controversy over Rational Expectations'
National Institute Economic Review, **96**, May: 53–61

In this short, nontechnical discussion of the contributions of RE, Mayes discusses all forms of modelling expectations. One drawback of the narrow form of RE, he claims, is that it conflicts with reality.

304   MCAULIFFE, Robert E. (1985)
'The Rational Expectations Hypothesis and Economic Analysis'
Eastern Economic Journal, **11** (4), October–December: 331–41

In this paper McAuliffe tries to separate the REH new classical

policy conclusions from the REH itself. He expresses great optimism regarding the future of RE in macroeconomics and financial
markets.

305   MCCAFFERTY, Stephen and Robert DRISKILL (1980)
       **'Problems of Existence and Uniqueness in Nonlinear Rational Expec-
       tations Models'**
       Econometrica, **48** (5), July: 1313–17

In this short paper the authors, building on Muth's work, deal with
problems of uniqueness and existence. Most macro models take
coefficients as given. But when one derives behavioural relationships
from optimizing behaviour, the coefficients become endogenous,
rendering the RE model *nonlinear*. Although such nonlinear models
are very difficult to compute, they are founded on optimizing behaviour.

306   MCCALLUM, Bennett T. (1984)
       'A Linearized Version of Lucas' Neutrality Model'
       Canadian Journal of Economics, **17** (1), February: 138–45

McCallum linearizes Lucas' original model. Despite problems with
RE, the result is quite easy to manipulate and retains the original
model's main properties.

307   MCCALLUM, Bennett T. (1983a)
       **'The Liquidity Trap and the Pigou Effect: A Dynamic Analysis with
       Rational Expectations'**
       Economica, **50** (200), November: 395–406

McCallum constructs a dynamic model of an economy with a
liquidity trap, a Pigou effect and RE. He examines whether a
tendency towards full employment values exists. He finds that if the
Pigou effect or a capital gains effect of expected inflation on disposable income is present, the system is well-behaved and stable.

308   MCCALLUM, Bennett T. (1983b)
       **'On Non-Uniqueness in Rational Expectations Models: An Attempt at
       Perspective'**

Journal of Monetary Economics, **11** (2), March: 139–68

This paper considers the problem of multiple solutions in RE models. McCallum argues that nonuniqueness is a property attributable not to the REH, but to dynamic models involving expectations in general. He introduces a procedure for finding the solution to a wide class of linear RE models which excludes the 'bubble or bootstrap effects' common to these models.

309   MCCALLUM, Bennett T. (1981a)
'The Current State of the Policy-Ineffectiveness Debate'
in Lucas and Sargent, 1981: 285–92

This article concentrates on the new classical policy ineffectiveness proposition. McCallum finds that the formal econometric evidence currently available – although unclear – is not inconsistent with the neutrality proposition.

310   MCCALLUM, Bennett T. (1981b)
'Price Level Determinacy with an Interest Rate Policy Rule and Rational Expectations'
Journal of Monetary Economics, **8** (3), November: 319–29

This is a discussion of Sargent-Wallace's (1975) conclusion that 'under an interest rate rule the price level is indeterminate' (p. 241 of '"Rational" Expectations, the Optimal Monetary Instrument, and the Optimal Money Supply Rule'). McCallum reconsiders this result and finds that, like the neutrality proposition, it does not apply to all interest-rate rules.

311   MCCALLUM, Bennett T. (1981c)
'Price-Level Stickiness and the Feasibility of Monetary Stabilization Policy with Rational Expectations'
in Lucas and Sargent, 1981: 277–84

McCallum here modifies a Sargent-Wallace model to incorporate stickiness. This change does not negate the Lucas-Sargent proposition that countercyclical monetary policy will be entirely ineffective if aggregate-supply fluctuations are initiated by informational errors and if economic agents' expectations are formed rationally. McCallum developed this model in response to complaints that the Lucas-Sargent neutrality proposition does not hold because prices are in reality sluggish, a fact which would eradicate the neutral property of the model.

312 MCCALLUM, Bennett T. (1980a)
'Rational Expectations and Macroeconomic Stabilization Policy: An Overview'
Journal of Money, Credit, and Banking, **12** (4), November: 716–46

McCallum describes the impact of the new classical stabilization analysis on macroeconomics in general. He does not try to provide a balanced account.

313 MCCALLUM, Bennett (1980b)
'The Significance of Rational Expectations Theory'
Challenge, **22**, January–February: 37–43
rpt in Martin Baily and Arthur M. Okun (eds.), *The Battle Against Unemployment and Inflation*
New York: Norton and Co., 1982: 144–52

The author discusses the significance of the new classical version of RE in an uncomplicated form.

314 MCCALLUM, Bennett T. (1979a)
'The Current State of the Policy-Ineffectiveness Debate'
American Economic Review: Papers and Proceedings, **69** (2), May: 240–5

Focusing on the Lucas-Sargent-Barro policy neutrality proposition, McCallum considers the major objections to it. After discussing the evidence – which is unclear – he concludes that the policy is not inconsistent with the neutrality proposition.

315 MCCALLUM, Bennett T. (1979b)
'Monetarism, Rational Expectations, Oligopolistic Pricing, and the MPS Econometric Model'
Journal of Political Economy, **87** (1), February: 57–73

Here McCallum considers the hypothesis that oligopolistic pricing behaviour will invalidate the Lucas-Sargent policy ineffectiveness proposition even if expectations are rational. He finds that this assertion depends upon the way in which lags are built into the price adjustment equation.

316   MCCALLUM, Bennett T. (1978a)
'Dating, Discounting, and the Robustness of the Lucas-Sargent Proposition'
Journal of Monetary Economics, **4** (1), January: 121–9

McCallum builds on the Lucas-Sargent policy inefficacy proposition that stabilization policy will be ineffective in an economy with an aggregate supply function which relates output to the difference between the current price level and the value expected during an earlier period. McCallum asks whether the neutrality proposition holds if the expectation of a *future* price is compared with the current actual price in the supply equation. He finds the answer to be yes, so long as the future price is discounted.

317   MCCALLUM, Bennett T. (1978b)
'Price Level Adjustments and the Rational Expectations Approach to Macroeconomic Stabilization Policy'
Journal of Money, Credit, and Banking, **10** (4), November: 418–36

McCallum modifies and extends his argument on price stickiness, adopting a new price adjustment mechanism. In his 1981(c) article the price level was sticky in relation to its anticipated value; here it is sticky in relation to the price level of the previous period. The equation is linear. Again he establishes the basic compatibility of sluggish price adjustment and the Lucas-Sargent neutrality proposition. These results are however confined to a particular model.

318   MCCALLUM, Bennett T. (1976a)
'Rational Expectations and the Estimation of Econometric Models'
International Economic Review, **17** (2), June: 484–90

McCallum argues that consistent estimators can be based on extrapolative predictors so long as one employs an instrumental variable estimation technique. This paper is a complement to C.R. Nelson's work.

319   MCCALLUM, Bennett T. (1976b)
'Rational Expectations and the Natural Rate Hypothesis'
Econometrica, **44** (1), January: 43–52

McCallum presents empirical results on the NRH based on a model
with RE.

320   MCCALLUM, Bennett T. (1975)
'Rational Expectations and the Natural Rate Hypothesis: Some Evidence for the United Kingdom'
Manchester School of Economics and Social Studies, **43** (1) March:
56–67

McCallum finds some evidence for the NRH, but not overwhelming
support.

321   MCCALLUM, Bennett T. (1972)
'Inventory Holdings, Rational Expectations, and the Law of Supply and Demand'
Journal of Political Economy, **80** (2), March–April: 386–93

Dissatisfaction has been expressed among economists that there is
no rationale underlying the 'law of supply and demand'. In this
paper McCallum shows that a plausible partial-equilibrium model
of an interperiod price-adjustment process with RE is consistent
with the law of supply and demand.

322   MCCALLUM, Bennett T. and J.K. WHITTAKER (1979)
'The Effectiveness of Fiscal Feedback Rules and Automatic Stabilizers under Rational Expectations'
Journal of Monetary Economics, **5**: 171–86

Most discussions of policy implications of RE centre on monetary
policy, but in this paper the authors add fiscal variables to the Lucas
model. They show that neutrality exists with respect to government
expenditure, but not with respect to automatic stabilizers. Fiscal
policy is more effective in a model with more than one good.

323   MCDONALD, John (1987)
'Muth's Concept of Rational Expectations'

Australian Economic Papers, **26** (49), December: 265–74

McDonald argues against Stegman's (1985) contention that the RE of a variable are always the expected value of the variable based on available information. Thus Stegman finds that RE are not always consistent with optimal behaviour. McDonald shows why this is inaccurate.

324   MCGEE, Robert T. and Richard T. STASIAK (1985)
'Does Anticipated Monetary Policy Matter?'
Journal of Money, Credit, and Banking, **17** (1), February: 16–27

After examining the policy ineffectiveness proposition of new classical writers, the authors offer an alternative method to handle the observational equivalence problem. They find that anticipated policy does influence output in the short run.

325   MCMAHON, Michael R. (1984a)
'An Appraisal of the New Classical Macroeconomics'
Journal of Macroeconomics, **6** (3), Summer: 335–46

McMahon appraises new classical economics within a Lakatosian framework of scientific research programmes. He concludes that new classical economics is a progressive scientific research programme.

326   MCMAHON, Michael R. (1984b)
'Expectations and Knowledge Assumptions in Some Popular Macroeconomics Models'
Atlantic Economic Journal, **12** (2), July: 68

In this one-page note, McMahon classifies expectations assumptions in macro models. When markets clear and all agents have the same – but incorrect – expectations we have the new classical macroeconomics of Lucas. When the same expectations assumption is combined with non-market clearing, we have the neoclassical synthesis represented by Klein or Patinkin. When agents have different expectations and markets clear, we have models from Wicksell and the early Keynes; when markets do not clear, we have the model in Keynes' *General Theory.*

327 MCNEES, Stephen K. (1978)
'The Rationality of Economic Forecasts'
American Economic Review, **68** (2), May: 301–305

McNees tests economic forecasts both for lack of bias and for any improvement on the basis of available information (i.e. for RE). He finds forecasts which are not rational for the period under study.

328 MEESE, Richard (1980)
'Dynamic Factor Demand Schedules for Labor and Capital under Rational Expectations'
Journal of Econometrics, **14** (1), Summer: 141–58

Meese combines a RE assumption with the adjustment cost approach to derive factor demand equations which are linear in the variables of the model. One advantage is that the model is not subject to Lucas' criticism of *ad hoc* estimation.

329 MELTZER, Allan H. (1984)
'Rational Expectations, Risk, Uncertainty, and Market Responses'
in Paul Wachtel (ed.), *Crises in the Economic and Financial Structure,*
Lexington, Mass./Toronto: Lexington Books, 1984: 3–22

Meltzer incorporates the Knight-Keynes concept of uncertainty into a RE model. He treats uncertainty as a shift in expected value following a shock to aggregate demand or supply.

330 MICHEL, Philippe (1983)
'Indétermination et détermination des prix en prévisions rationelles'
('Price Determinacy and Indeterminacy in Rational Expectations Models')
Economie appliquée, **36** (1): 77–97

Considering the problem of price indeterminacy in RE models, Michel examines five models from the literature. He finds that the assumption that expectations are bounded often suffices to determine a solution. This assumption is arbitrary in some models, justified in others.

331   MILGROM, Paul R. (1981)
'**Rational Expectations, Information Acquisition, and Competitive Bidding**'
Econometrica, **49** (4), June: 921–43

Milgrom argues that most RE market equilibrium models do not provide for price information. He thus develops a bidding model where bidders act as price takers and where prices do convey information.

332   MILLS, Edwin S. (1957)
'**Theory of Inventory Decision**'
Econometrica, **25**, April: 222–8

In this paper Mills introduces his notion of 'implicit expectations' which are further developed in his book *Prices, Output and Inventory Policy* (1962). Implicit expectations are so closely related to RE that Mills deserves to be credited with developing the concept.

333   MINFORD, Patrick (1986)
'**Rational Expectations and Monetary Policy**'
Scottish Journal of Political Economy, **33** (4), November: 317–33

In this paper Minford examines how the implications of RE have changed the way economists think about monetary policy. Money, contracts and assets are more of a mystery than ever because they are difficult to reconcile with rational behaviour within RE models. Hence no firm foundation for a theory of monetary policy yet exists.

334   MINFORD, Patrick (1981)
'**Dynamic Predictive Tests of a Rational Expectations Model of the U.K.**'
British Review of Economic Issues, **3** (9), Autumn: 39–50

Minford discusses the tests carried out on the 'Liverpool model' of the UK economy, concluding that it does forecast accurately and does support rational over adaptive expectations.

335   MINFORD, Patrick, M. BRECH and Kent MATTHEWS (1980)
'**A Rational Expectations Model of the U.K. under Floating Exchange Rates**'

European Economic Review, **14**: 189–219

By first constructing a model of an open economy with trade and capital flows and then incorporating a narrow version of RE into it, the authors find that the model is unstable due to RE. Their result that unemployment does not settle at a natural rate when expectations of inflation are realized is unusual in a RE model – due to the theory of wage and price setting they incorporate. Money is not neutral in the new classical sense.

336   MINFORD, Patrick, Kent MATTHEWS and Satwant MAR-WAHA (1979)
'Terminal Conditions as a Means of Ensuring Unique Solutions for Rational Expectations Models with Forward Expectations'
Economics Letters, **4**: 117–20

The authors discuss problems of multiple solution paths in RE models. They impose terminal conditions on such models to find a unique solution, arguing that this method is superior to imposing a stability condition.

337   MINFORD, A.P.L. and D.A. PEEL (1983)
'Some Implications of Partial Current Information Sets in Macroeconomic Models Embodying Rational Expectations'
Manchester School of Economics and Social Studies, **51** (3), September: 235–49

The authors consider what happens in two simple macro models if agents' information sets include observations of current macroeconomic variables. They find that the procedure of solving RE models on an information set dated at time t is wrong because agents observe *some* current global information. Partial information affects the properties of RE and should not be neglected,

338   MINFORD, Patrick and David PEEL (1982)
'The Microfoundations of the Phillips Curve with Rational Expectations'
Oxford Economic Papers, **34** (3), November: 449–51

The authors discuss Lipsey and Phelps' augmented Phillips curve and RE. They find that the disequilibrium microfoundations of the Phillips curve cannot be sustained when agents know the model and utilize *all* available information. Thus they argue that it 'is no theoretical accident that Phillips curves used in RE models have generally been based on equilibrium microfoundations' (p. 451). They warn against interpreting RE Phillips curves as part of the Phillips-Lipsey-Phelps tradition.

339   MINFORD, Patrick and David PEEL (1981)
       'The Role of Monetary Stabilization Policy under Rational Expectations'
       Manchester School of Economics and Social Studies, **49** (1), March: 39–50

Exploring monetary stabilization policy in models incorporating the REH, the authors show that a small change in the model underlying the REH allows a monetary feedback rule to be effective. They change the aggregate supply hypothesis rather than assume contracts and conclude that RE do not rule out countercyclical policy.

340   MINFORD, A.P.L. and D.A. PEEL (1980)
       'The Natural Rate Hypothesis and Rational Expectations – A Critique of Some Recent Developments'
       Oxford Economic Papers, **32** (1): 71–81

The authors consider the Lucas interpretation of the Phillips curve as a relation between transitory inflation and unemployment where the labour market is always in equilibrium. They argue that this approach needs careful definition with respect to the REH. Clarifying the two versions of the Lucas relationship in the literature, they conclude that – given RE – there are difficulties with both versions.

341   MISHKIN, Frederic S. (1982a)
       'Does Anticipated Aggregate Demand Policy Matter? Further Econometric Results'
       American Economic Review, **72** (4), September: 788–802

In this paper Mishkin tests the policy neutrality proposition of the new classical economists. The empirical evidence does not support the proposition that only unanticipated aggregate demand policy matters. The NRH is rejected but not the REH.

342 MISHKIN, Frederic S. (1982b)
'Does Anticipated Monetary Policy Matter? An Econometric Investigation'
Journal of Political Economy, **90** (1): 22–51

Concentrating on the policy neutrality result of new classical economics, Mishkin develops a method for empirically analysing RE models displaying the neutrality proposition. In answering his own question, he finds that anticipated monetary policy does matter. The neutrality proposition was rejected, but the REH fared somewhat better. A joint test of the two components produced a strong rejection.

343 MISHKIN, Frederic S. (1981)
'Are Market Forecasts Rational?'
American Economic Review, **71** (3), June: 295–306

Here Mishkin tests the rationality of inflation rates and of short-term interest rates in bond markets. His empirical tests show that the bond market is rational.

344 MITCHELL, Douglas W. (1982)
'The Optimal Policy Rule under Rational Expectations and Multiplier Uncertainty'
Journal of Economics and Business, **34** (2): 129–33

Mitchell combines the literature on RE with that on optimal policy under conditions of multiplier uncertainty. He shows that policy does make a difference with regard to RE because it affects price-level (instead of the usual output) variance.

345 MODIGLIANI, Franco and Robert J. SHILLER (1973)
'Inflation, Rational Expectations and the Term Structure of Interest Rates'
Economica, N.S., **40** (157), February: 12–43

The authors aim to generalize the approach that – to a remarkable extent – explains the behaviour of the term structure of interest rates; this is done by combining the 'preferred habitat' version of expectations with a model of their formation in which expected future rates are a linear function of past rates. They find that the model performs well and satisfies the conditions for rationality.

346   MOOSA, S.A. (1983)
'The Treatment of Uncertainty in the Application of Rational Expectations to the Analysis of Economic Policy'
Applied Economics, **15** (4), August: 451–8

Although classical macroeconomic RE models have made a contribution by emphasizing that the public cannot be fooled forever, this has been overstated. Moosa points out that the reactions of risk-averse economic agents to higher moments of the distribution of forecast errors should be incorporated into the models. Without their inclusion, the information set may be misspecified.

347   MORK, Knut Anton (1985)
'Factor Substitution, Rational Expectations, and the Effects of Commodity Price Shocks on Employment and Investment'
Economic Inquiry, **23** (3), July: 507–24

Mork finds that substitution elasticities and technological parameters are of crucial importance for understanding commodity price shocks in a RE model.

348   MULDER, Christian (1988)
'Testing Korteweg's Rational Expectations Model for a Small Open Economy'
De Economist, **136** (1), March: 22–49

Mulder discusses Korteweg's model, providing evidence to refute many of his conclusions.

349   MULLINEAUX, Donald J. (1980)
'Inflation Expectations and Money Growth in the United States'
American Economic Review, **70** (1), March: 149–61

The author tests models that explain the process by which forecasters anticipate inflation. Using Carlson's (1977) data, he tests for rationality – defined as forecasts which 'efficiently incorporate "available" information' (p. 158). Mullineaux is not able to reject the hypothesis that the data satisfy rationality.

350 MULLINEAUX, Donald J. (1978)
'On Testing for Rationality: Another Look at the Livingston Price Expectations Data'
Journal of Political Economy, **86** (2), Part 2: 329–36

In this paper the author exposes the weaknesses of the tests carried out by Pesando (1975) and Carlson (1977) on price expectations data. He changes their tests and – contrary to their own conclusions – finds that the Carlson data pass, but that the Pesando data fail, the rationality test.

351 MUSSA, Michael (1978)
'On the Inherent Stability of Rationally Adaptive Expectations'
Journal of Monetary Economics, **4** (2), April: 307–13

Mussa reconsiders Cagan's model of hyperinflation by changing the assumption of adaptive to rational expectations. Whereas Cagan found that inflation can accelerate under adaptive expectations, under Mussa's assumption RE yield a stable system.

352 MUTH, John F. (1981a)
'Estimation of Economic Relationships Containing Latent Expectations Variables'
in Lucas and Sargent, 1981: 321–8

If expectations are rational, how can a model be estimated from observable data? Without great difficulty, according to Muth. This paper was written in 1960 and foreshadows much of his later work.

353 MUTH, John F. (1981b)
'Optimal Properties of Exponentially Weighted Forecasts'
Journal of the American Statistical Association, **55** (290)
rpt in Lucas and Sargent, 1981: 23–31

Muth argues that an exponentially weighted average can be defined as the value of a time series with transitory and permanent components, i.e., as a random walk with noise. He applies this to Friedman's permanent income hypothesis.

354   MUTH, John F. (1961)
'Rational Expectations and the Theory of Price Movements'
Econometrica, **29** (3), July: 315–35
rpt in Lucas and Sargent, 1981: 3–22

This paper marks the very beginning of RE. The REH is discussed and applied to the cobweb model.

355   NELSON, Charles (1975a)
'Rational Expectations and the Estimation of Econometric Models'
International Economic Review, **16** (3), October: 555–61

Nelson discusses the use of RE in econometric models. He argues that the source of inconsistency in regressions where RE are replaced by extrapolative expectations is different from that in the usual models which allow for errors in variables.

356   NELSON, Charles R. (1975b)
'Rational Expectations and the Predictive Efficiency of Economic Models'
Journal of Business, **48** (3), July: 331–43

Nelson argues that 'rational' should not be understood simply as a synonym for 'unbiased' or 'optimal extrapolative'. Some writers now recognize that agents may draw on an information set wider than the past history of the variable being considered. Nelson first examines the circumstances under which a larger information set will be relevant for the formation of RE and then evaluates the payoff to RE agents from a knowledge of economic structure.

357   NERLOVE, Marc (1983)
'Expectations, Plans, and Realizations in Theory and Practice'
Econometrica, **51** (5), September: 1251–79

Nerlove analyses data from German and French firms on expectation formation, finding major differences between them. Models of expectation formation and planning (of which RE is a part) are well presented and discussed.

358   NISHIJIMA, Shoji (1984)
'Indexing Policies and Macroeconomic Stability in Brazil: Rational Expectation Model'
Kobe Economic Business Review, **30**: 73–86

The author develops a stochastic RE model to analyse the effect of RE on price and output variance. Testing the random walk hypothesis derived from the model on Brazilian data, he finds evidence in its support.

359   NISHIMURA, Kiyohiko G. (1986)
'Rational Expectations and Price Rigidity in a Monopolistically Competitive Market'
Review of Economic Studies, **53** (2), April: 283–92

The author examines a log-linear model of a monopolistically competitive market with RE subject to demand and cost disturbances. Prices are rigid due to incomplete information on the seller's side. When information is incomplete, competition makes the average price insensitive to short-run changes in demand and cost, although firms form RE about market-wide disturbances. Thus the complete and incomplete information cases have wholly different effects on price behaviour.

360   NOBLE, Nicholas R. (1982)
'Granger Causality and Expectational Rationality: A Note'
Journal of Money, Credit, and Banking, **14** (4), November, Part 1: 532–7

In this note Noble examines the implications of the REH for price expectations (inflation) within the context of Nelson's testing methods. He argues that Nelson's evidence derives from a misspecified Lucas aggregate supply equation and not from the particular way in which expectations are formed.

361   OBSTFELD, Maurice (1981)
'Capital Mobility and Devaluation in an Optimizing Model with Rational Expectations'

American Economic Review: Papers and Proceedings, **71** (2), May: 217–21

Obstfeld examines the effects of exchange-rate policies in a model in which individuals with RE maximize lifetime utility.

362   OKUN, Arthur M. (1980)
'Rational-Expectations-with-Misperceptions as a Theory of the Business Cycle'
Journal of Money, Credit, and Banking, **12** (4), November, Part 2: 817–25

Okun argues that new classical economics provides a 'logically satisfactory but empirically unsatisfactory explanation of the business cycle' (p. 832). He believes that the assumption of continuous market clearing must be dropped in order to develop a realistic alternative.

363   ORMEROD, Paul (1982)
'Rational and Non-Rational Explanations of Inflation in Wage Equations for the United Kingdom'
Economica, **49** (196), November: 375–87

Comparing different methods of expectations formation, Ormerod finds that the RE model has the greatest explanatory power, but not significantly more than alternative specifications. He concludes that there is no major advantage to using RE.

364   OROSEL, Gerhard O. (1985)
'Infinite Horizon Rational Expectations Equilibrium in a Competitive Market for an Exhaustible Resource'
International Economic Review, **26** (3), October: 701–20

Orosel analyses the competitive equilibrium of a market for an exhaustible resource under the assumption that demand is stochastic, suppliers are risk-neutral, expectations are rational, and the time horizon is infinite. He finds a unique RE equilibrium; also that short-run demand shocks do not have much influence on price.

365   OTANI, Kiyoshi (1985)
'Rational Expectations and Nonneutrality of Money'

Weltwirtschaftliches Archiv, **121** (2): 203–16

Otani criticizes the new classical assumption that money is neutral when information is perfect, expectations are rational, and there is no money illusion. The author refutes this assumption, using the Lucas models of 1972 and 1973 and the Barro model of 1976. He shows that nonneutrality – not neutrality – tends to be the rule.

366 OXLEY, Leslie T. (1983)
'Rational Expectations and Macroeconomic Policy: A Review Article'
Scottish Journal of Political Economy, **30** (2), June: 181–91

Oxley reviews Begg (1980), Lucas and Sargent (1981), Fischer (1980) and several other works on monetarism and money. He also outlines the concept and history of the RE school.

367 PASHIGIAN, B. Peter (1970)
'Rational Expectations and the Cobweb Theory'
Journal of Political Economy, **78** (2), March–April: 338–52

The author presents a cobweb model with RE to investigate price fluctuations. His model shows that adaptive expectations closely approximate rational expectations.

368 PATTERSON, K.D. (1987)
'The Development of Expectations Generating Schemes which are Asymptotically Rational'
Scottish Journal of Political Economy, **34** (1), February: 1–18

Patterson designs expectations-generating schemes which prevent agents from making systematic mistakes in the long run. He develops the concept of asymptotic rationality.

369 PEARLMAN, Joseph, David CURRIE and Paul LEVINE (1986)
'Rational Expectations Models with Partial Information'
Economic Modelling, **3** (2), April: 90–105

The authors provide a general solution to the problem of partial information in linear discrete time stochastic RE models. They compare the partial with the full information case.

370   PEEL, D.A. and J.S. METCALFE (1979)
'Divergent Expectations and the Dynamic Stability of Some Simple Macro Economic Models'
Economic Journal, **83** (356), December: 789–98

The authors investigate the implications for a macro model if the assumption that price expectations are formed in the same manner in different markets is relaxed. They show that when at least one set of agents forms expectations adaptively while the rest form them rationally, the economy behaves as if all expectations were adaptive.

371   PERSSON, Mats (1979)
'Rational Expectations in Log Linear Models'
Scandinavian Journal of Economics, **81** (3): 378–86

The author shows that real output can be affected systematically by monetary policy even if expectations are formed rationally in the Muth-Lucas sense. He concludes that the way in which aggregate supply is calculated in econometric models – as a log-linear function – is inappropriate because it implies that average real output increases monotonically with any variance in the money supply rule.

372   PESANDO, James E. (1976)
'Rational Expectations and Distributed Lag Expectation Proxies'
Journal of the American Statistical Association, **71** (353), March: 36–42

Pesando reviews the properties of RE in the context of autoregressive forecasting – the expectations-generating mechanism implicit in the use of distributed lag proxies. He then tests the REH on a set of directly observed expectations data. He concludes that research with RE is encouraging, although the REH may be too stringent a requirement to impose on distributed lag proxies.

373   PESANDO, James E. (1975)
'A Note on the Rationality of Livingston Price Expectations'
Journal of Political Economy, **83**: 849–58

In this note Pesando discusses previous findings and problems of rationality and price expectations. He concludes that the fact that

Livingston price expectations are not rational casts doubt on the assumption that they represent market forecasts. If one insists that they are, one must conclude that market forecasts of inflation are not rational.

374   PESARAN, M.H. (1986)
'The New Classical Macroeconomics: A Critical Exposition'
Economics Reprint No. 111, University of Cambridge Department of Applied Economics
rpt in F. van der Ploeg (ed.) *Mathematical Methods in Economics,*
Chichester, New York, etc.: John Wiley and Sons Ltd, 1984, pp. 195–215.

Pesaran discusses the 'two basic building blocks of the new classical macroeconomic models' – the REH and NRH. He then incorporates these two hypotheses into a simple IS-LM model, showing how the policy neutrality proposition follows. He stresses the extreme nature of new classical assumptions and their limitations, then sums up the usefulness of the policy neutrality proposition: it is a 'theoretical curiosity' (p. 213).

375   PESARAN, M.H. (1985)
'Formation of Inflation Expectations in British Manufacturing Industries'
Economic Journal, **95**, December: 948–75

Pesaran investigates the way inflation expectations are formed in British manufacturing industries. He finds random errors, invalidating serial independence of forecast errors as implied by the REH. The orthogonality property is also rejected, and overall results are mixed.

376   PESARAN, M.H. (1984)
'Expectations Formations and Macroeconometric Modelling', with comments by C. Gourieroux and Jean Tirole
in Pierre Malgrange and Pierre-Alain Muet (eds.), *Contemporary Macroeconomic Modelling*
Oxford: Basil Blackwell, 1984: 27–61

Pesaran investigates RE and uncertainty (stemming from ignorance of other agents' decisions). He argues that when the decision-making process is dominated by this type of uncertainty, RE in their narrow form are inadequate. He then suggests direct measurements of expectations (also advocated by Katona) and proposes methods of converting survey data into quantitative measurements of expectations.

377   PESARAN, M.H. (1982)
'A Critique of the Proposed Tests of the Natural Rate-Rational Expectations Hypothesis'
Economic Journal, **92**, September: 529–54

In this discussion Pesaran focuses on the results of tests of the REH-NRH made by new classical economists. Pesaran finds that a Keynesian model is more consistent with the facts.

378   PESARAN, M.H. (1981)
'Identification of Rational Expectations Models'
Journal of Econometrics, **16**: 375–98

Pesaran considers the identification problem of simultaneous RE models. He concludes that identification is extremely difficult because economists can never be in possession of the type of *a priori* information needed to identify the models. Thus he does not think that RE models can be distinguished empirically from non-RE models and vice-versa.

379   PHELPS, Edmund S. (1983)
'The Trouble with "Rational Expectations" and the Problem of Inflation Stabilization', with comment by P. Cagan
in Frydman and Phelps, 1983: 31–45

Phelps discusses problems connected with the extreme-information assumption. He replaces RE with a more general theory which allows agents to believe that other agents' expectations differ from their own. He applies this to a model whose goal is to retard inflation without causing a recession.

380   PHELPS, Edmund S. and John B. TAYLOR (1977)
'Stabilizing Powers of Monetary Policy under Rational Expectations'

Journal of Political Economy, **85** (1): 163–90

Assuming sticky prices and wages, the authors show that monetary policy can stabilize the economy in a RE model.

381   PINDYCK, Robert S. and Julio J. ROTEMBERG (1983)
'Dynamic Factor Demands under Rational Expectations'
Scandinavian Journal of Economics, **85** (2): 223–38

The authors develop a RE model in which they analyse the way in which tax changes, changes in relative prices and changes in aggregate output all affect investment and employment over time.

382   PLOTT, Charles R. and Shyam SUNDER (1982)
'Efficiency of Experimental Security Markets with Insider Information: An Application to Rational-Expectations Models'
Journal of Political Economy, **90** (4), August: 663–98

The authors report on the behaviour of five markets created in a laboratory environment to explore various theoretical implications of insider information. They find that the markets behave as predicted by RE equilibrium models.

383   POOLE, William (1980)
'Macroeconomic Policy, 1971–75: An Appraisal', with comment by James L. Pierce and discussion
in Fischer, 1980: 269–84

Poole appraises macroeconomic policies from 1971–75, discussing the issue of which is more effective – rules or authority – when executing monetary policy (the new classical decision favours rules). Poole concludes that rules would have been better than the policy adopted at that time.

384   POOLE, William (1976)
'Rational Expectations in the Macro Model'
Brooking Papers on Economic Activity, **2**: 463–505

Poole explores the implication of the REH for macro and business cycle theories. He concludes that new classical theory has 'provided much more insight into the failures of empirical macro models than into the construction of successful ones' (p. 505).

385 PRECIOUS, Mark (1985)
'Demand Constraints, Rational Expectations and Investment Theory'
Oxford Economic Papers, **37** (4), December: 576–605

Precious extends a popular model of the firm (the 'q' model of investment) to incorporate the possibility of disequilibrium and regime switching. He assumes that expectations are rational.

386 PRITCHETT, David V. (1976)
'Econometric Policy Evaluation: A Critique-Comment'
Journal of Monetary Economics, Supplementary Series I: 63–4

The author discusses Lucas' famous paper on policy evaluation. He agrees that the modelling of the Phillips curve is inappropriate, but he finds Lucas' alternative unsatisfactory as well.

387 PUDNEY, S.E. (1982)
'The Identification of Rational Expectations Models under Structural Neutrality'
Journal of Economic Dynamics and Control, **4** (1), February: 117–21

In this note the author shows that the parameters measuring the strength of response to unanticipated shocks in the structural neutrality version of the linear RE model cannot be identified unless the covariance properties of the structural disturbances are restricted.

388 RADNER, Roy (1979)
'Rational Expectations Equilibrium: Generic Existence and the Information Revealed by Prices'
Econometrica, **47** (3), May: 655–78

Radner shows that RE equilibria exist that reveal all of the initial information to all traders provided that the number of alternative states of initial information is finite.

389 RAMB, Bernd-Thomas (1984)
'Ineffektivität der Wirtschaftspolitik bei "rationalen Erwartungen"?
Eine unkorrekte, aber auch modellspezifische Behauptung' ('Ineffec-
tiveness of Economic Policy under "Rational Expectations"? An
Incorrect but Model-Specific Assertion')
Kredit und Kapital, 17 (2): 165–79

As the title of this paper indicates, the focus is on the policy ineffectiveness result. Ramb shows that the ineffectiveness thesis is not a
generalized result, but one specific to the model. (See Maussner for a
critique of this paper.)

390 RAMSER, Hans J. (1978)
'Rationale Erwartungen und Wirtschaftspolitik' ('Rational Expec-
tations and Economic Policy')
Zeitschrift für die gesamte Staatswissenschaft, 134 (1), March: 57–72

Also dealing with the policy ineffectiveness of new classical models,
Ramser shows that this property is specific to the model.

391 RAVILLION, Martin (1986)
'On Expectations Formation When Future Welfare Is Contemplated?'
Kyklos, 39 (4): 564–73

This is a general discussion of expectations, of which RE are a part.
The author argues that the narrow version of RE restricts the
derived preference ordering of expectations and thus excludes reflec-
tion about the future.

392 REDSLOB, A. (1983)
'Rationalité des anticipations et théorie de la politique monétaire: une
note critique' ('Rational Expectations Hypothesis and the Theory of
Monetary Policy: A Critical Note')
Economies et sociétés, 17 (7–8), July–August: 1259–75

Redslob discusses the new classical approach to monetary policy
and the neutrality proposition of new classical economists. He criticizes the long-run nature of the model.

393 REVANKAR, Nagesh S. (1980)
'Testing of the Rational Expectations Hypothesis'

Econometrica, **48** (6), September: 1347–63

The author develops a test of RE and discusses estimation problems.

394   RODRIGUEZ, Carlos Alfredo (1978)
'A Simple Keynesian Model of Inflation and Unemployment under Rational Expectations'
Weltwirtschaftliches Archiv, **114** (1): 1–11

This paper analyses a simple Keynesian model of inflation and unemployment when expectations are rational. He shows how the economy can be stabilized using monetary policy.

395   ROGERS, C. (1982)
'Rational Expectations and Neoclassical Economics: The Methodology of the New Classical Macroeconomics'
South African Journal of Economics, **50** (4), December: 318–39

In this paper Rogers investigates new classical economics from a very critical standpoint.

396   ROTEMBERG, Julio J. (1984)
'Interpreting the Statistical Failures of Some Rational Expectations Macroeconomc Models'
American Economic Review, **74** (2), May: 188–93

Rotemberg assesses the economic importance of statistical rejections of empirical RE models – the fact that data lead to different estimates. He shows that such statistical rejections have economic meaning for some models in that the difference between the various estimates is large.

397   ROUZAUD, Catherine (1983)
'Anticipations rationnelles et information révélée par les prix: une introduction'
Revue économique, **34** (6), November: 1116–44

Rouzaud discusses RE and information revealed by prices. She extends the Arrow-Debreu model, assuming identical information for all agents, and then introduces differentiated information of agents. Finally, equilibrium with RE and information revealed by price are considered. She also reviews much of the American literature.

398 RUNDE, J. and C. TORR (1985)
'Divergent Expectations and Rational Expectations'
South African Journal of Economics, **53** (3), September: 217–25

The authors make a case for 'divergent expectations' and against rational expectations.

399 RUTHERFORD, Malcolm (1984)
'Rational Expectations and Keynesian Uncertainty: A Critique'
Journal of Post Keynesian Economics, **6** (3), Spring: 377–87

Comparing Keynes' position on expectations with RE, Rutherford concludes that RE are flawed, but so are all other formulations of expectations.

400 SAINT-ETIENNE, Christian (1984)
'De l'importance réelle de l'hypothese de la rationalité des anticipations' ('On the Real Importance of the REH')
Revue d'économie politique, **94** (6), November–December: 773–91

The author reviews the concept and shows that the REH is necessary to eliminate free parameters from dynamic systems.

401 SALEMI, Michael K. (1979)
'Adaptive Expectations, Rational Expectations, and Money Demand in Hyperinflation in Germany'
Journal of Monetary Economics, **5** (4), October: 593–604

Salemi reconsiders Sargent and Wallace's conclusions in their study of money demand in Germany during the era of hyperinflation (see Lucas and Sargent, 1981: book, pp. 429–52 and Sargent, 1986: book). He rejects the proposition that expectations are rational.

402 SALEMI, Michael K. and Thomas J. SARGENT (1979)
'The Demand for Money during Hyperinflation under Rational Expectations: II'

International Economic Review, **20** (3), October: 741–58

In this paper the authors estimate and test Cagan's model for the special case in which his adaptive expectations mechanism coincides with RE. The evidence for RE is not very strong.

403   SARGENT, Thomas J. (1982)
'Beyond Demand and Supply Curves in Macroeconomics'
American Economic Review: Papers and Proceedings, **72** (2), May: 382–9

In this paper Sargent sketches the development of RE in macroeconometrics.

404   SARGENT, Thomas J. (1981)
'Interpreting Economic Time Series'
Journal of Political Economy, **89** (2), April: 213–48

Sargent explores the econometric implications for the assumption that people's observed behaviour changes if their constraints change. Sargent argues that the model also changes when constraints change, a factor which should be taken into account.

405   SARGENT, Thomas J. (1979)
'A Note on Maximum Likelihood Estimation of the Rational Expectations Model of the Term Structure'
Journal of Monetary Economics, **5** (1): 133–43

In this paper Sargent observes that the RE theory of the term structure of interest rates allows certain sequences of forward interest rates to be modelled as martingales. An approach taken by Modigliani, Sutch and Shiller, Sargent modifies it by estimating the vector autoregression of long and short rates.

406   SARGENT, Thomas J. (1978a)
'Estimation of Dynamic Labor Demand Schedules under Rational Expectations'
Journal of Political Economy, **86** (6): 1039–44

Sargent estimates a linear demand schedule for labour. He re-examines the Dunlop-Tarshis-Keynes exchange within the framework of a RE model.

407   SARGENT, Thomas J. (1978b)
'Rational Expectations, Econometric Exogeneity, and Consumption'
Journal of Political Economy, **86** (4), August: 673–700

In this work Sargent focuses on Friedman's permanent-income model of consumption, obtaining estimates for US data within a RE framework. The empirical evidence is 'discouraging'.

408   SARGENT, Thomas J. (1976)
'A Classical Macro-econometric Model for the United States'
Journal of Political Economy, **84** (2), April: 207–37

In this paper Sargent proposes a statistical definition of the NRH and then tests it using a model which has the new classical policy implication of neutrality. His aim is to test how firmly the data reject a model incorporating strong new classical properties. The evidence for rejection, he finds, is not 'overwhelming and decisive' (p. 236).

409   SARGENT, Thomas J. (1973a)
'"Rational Expectations": A Correction'
Brookings Papers on Economic Activity, **3**: 799–800

This is an amendment to his 1973(b) article. Sargent corrects his regression computations, which were lagged four more quarters than reported.

410   SARGENT, Thomas J. (1973b)
'Rational Expectations, the Real Rate of Interest, and the Natural Rate of Unemployment', with comments by David Fand and Stephen Goldfeld and discussion
Brookings Papers on Economic Activity, **2**: 429–80

Sargent presents a macroeconomic model in which a version of Irving Fisher's theory of the relationship between interest rates and expected inflation is correct. The implications for the model are typically 'Chicago-school'. One test rejects the NRH.

411   SARGENT, Thomas J. and Neil WALLACE (1975)
'"Rational" Expectations, the Optimal Monetary Instruments, and the Optimal Money Supply Rule'
Journal of Political Economy, **83** (2), April: 241–54

The authors analyse alternative monetary policies in an *ad hoc* model with RE. The model incorporates the Lucas supply function because of its microeconomic foundations. They find that output is independent of the money-supply rule, while the price level is indeterminate under an interest-rate rule.

412   SAUNDERS, Peter (1983)
'A Disaggregate Study of the Rationality of Australian Producers' Price Expectations'
Manchester School of Economics and Social Studies, **51** (4): 380–98

Saunders assesses the empirical validity of the REH using data on Australian producers' price expectations. He finds that such data are not unbiased in most industries. The REH is clearly rejected in three industries, cannot be rejected in three others and is inconclusive for the remaining six. He concludes that the burden of proof lies with the RE theorists.

413   SCARTH, William M. (1985)
'A Note on Non-Uniqueness in Rational Expectations Models'
Journal of Monetary Economics, **15** (2), January: 247–54

In this note Scarth suggests a procedure to improve McCallum's (1983(b)) method for solving linear RE models.

414   SHACKLE, G.L.S. (1984)
'Comment on Papers by Randall Bausor and Malcolm Rutherford'
('Toward a Historically Dynamic Economics: Examples and Illustrations' and 'Rational Expectations and Keynesian Uncertainty: A Critique')
Journal of Post Keynesian Economics, **6** (3), Spring: 388–93

In a review of these two papers by Bausor and Rutherford, Shackle takes a very critical view of the narrow version of RE.

415 SHAH, Anup (1983)
'Rational Expectations Macro Models with Possible Steady-State Inflation and Unemployment'
Journal of Macroeconomics, **5** (4), Fall: 461–71

Shah presents a RE model. Starting from a disequilibrium situation either of the Keynesian type or of the demand-inflation type in which money is nonneutral, he demonstrates that the economy converges to equilibrium with market clearing. The new classical model, however, yields a situation in which labour markets remain out of equilibrium.

416 SHAW, G.K. (1987)
'Rational Expectations'
Bulletin of Economic Research, **39** (3), July: 187–209

In this useful recent introduction to RE, Shaw discusses the movement's development within the recent history of macroeconomics. Since equations are avoided, nonmathematical economists as well as noneconomists are well served.

417 SHEEHY, Edmund J. (1984)
'Money and Output in Latin America: Some Tests of a Rational Expectations Approach'
Journal of Developmental Economics, **14** (1–2), January–February: 203–18

Using a Barro model, Sheehy tests for the relationship between money and output in 16 Latin American countries. He finds that money growth is anticipated to a large extent. (Studies by Barro and Hanson of money and output in Latin America came to different conclusions.)

418 SHILLER, Robert J. (1980)
'Can the Fed Control Real Interest Rates?'
in Fischer, 1980: 117–67

This paper focuses solely on interest rates and the monetary authority's ability to control them. Discussing three hypotheses about the Fed's range of controls, the evidence suggests that it should have some ability to control expected real interest rates.

419   SHILLER, Robert J. (1978)
'Rational Expectations and the Dynamic Structure of Macroeconomic Models: A Critical Review'
Journal of Monetary Economics, **4** (1), January: 1–44

This critical technical survey of the literature on RE and macroeconomic dynamic models is recommended to anyone learning about RE. In particular, Shiller considers the NRH, optimal linear forecasts, general linear RE models, and information and convergence problems in RE models.

420   SHILLER, Robert J. (1973)
'Rational Expectations and the Term Structure of Interest Rates, A Comment'
Journal of Money, Credit, and Banking, **5**: 856–60

Shiller discusses the limitations of Sargent's (1972) model of the term structure of interest rates. Shiller is concerned with two restrictive assumptions: that available information is assumed to consist only of the past history of interest rates, and that forecasting rules are linear.

421   SIMON, Herbert A. (1984)
'On the Behavioral and Rational Foundations of Economic Dynamics'
Journal of Behavior and Organization, **5** (1), March: 35–55

This is a general discussion of rationality and business cycle theory. Simon makes a case for steering RE in the behaviouralist direction, suggesting that we should pay more attention to the way expectations are formed.

422   SIMON, Herbert A. (1978)
'Rationality as Process and as Product of Thought'
American Economic Review: Papers and Proceedings, **68** (2), May: 1–16

This article focuses on rationality in general and not only on RE. However, RE are considered within the widest scope of economics and the social sciences, providing perspective on the new theoretical tool. Simon argues that RE do not correspond to any classical criterion of rationality and thus would be better labelled 'consistent expectations'.

423 SIMS, Christopher A. (1980)
'Macroeconomics and Reality'
Econometrica, **48** (1), January: 1–48

Sims summarizes objections to various approaches to econometric analysis, arguing that the models are in fact not overidentified as assumed. The REH forms part of this discussion.

424 SINGH, Harinder (1986)
'When Are Expectations Rational? Some Vexing Questions and Behavioral Clues'
Journal of Behavioral Economics, **15** (1/2), Spring–Summer: 191–209

This is another nontechnical introduction to RE. Singh makes a case for incorporating knowledge from empirical psychology, giving examples of how economics could benefit.

425 SINHA, Dipendra (1988)
'Irrational Expectations, Unclearing Markets and a Business Cycle That Won't Go Away: The Recent School of New Classical Economists Comes a Cropper on Basic Economic Facts'
American Journal of Economics and Sociology, **47** (3), July: 345–54

New classical economics is investigated and assessed quite negatively.

426 SINN, Hans-Werner (1984)
'Rationale Erwartungen, Rationierung und Rezession – Braucht keynesianische Politik dumme Bürger?' ('Rational Expectations, Rationing, and Recession – Does Keynesian Policy Need Dull Citizens?')
Jahrbücher für Nationalökonmie und Statistik, **199** (2), February: 158–78

Sinn presents a model of the labour and goods market underlying RE models. Examining the West German market, he finds that the RE literature does not explain German unemployment. He defends policy effectiveness.

427   SMALL, David H. (1979)
      'Unanticipated Money Growth and Unemployment in the United States: Comment'
      American Economic Review, **69** (5), December: 996–1003

      Small argues that the new classical models are at odds with the evidence. He rejects Barro's monetary model in favour of something more flexible.

428   SNIPPE, Jan (1986)
      'Varieties of Rational Expectations: Their Differences and Relations'
      Journal of Post Keynesian Economics, **8** (3), Spring: 427–37

      This article treats the varieties of RE in macro and microeconomics.

429   SNOWER, Dennis J. (1984)
      'Rational Expectations, Nonlinearities, and the Effectiveness of Monetary Policy'
      Oxford Economic Papers, **36** (2), June: 177–99

      Snower shows that the NRH and REH do not necessarily yield the policy neutrality hypothesis. He argues that the linear models of the new classical economists do not rest on solid foundations.

430   SOLOW, Robert M. (1980)
      'What to Do (Macroeconomically) When OPEC Comes', with a comment by Neil Wallace
      in Fischer, 1980: 249–67

      Solow's assignment is to state the correct macroeconomic (monetary and fiscal) policy for 1974–75. His basis for this evaluation is a non-market-clearing model which is not restricted by the NRH or the REH.

431   SPEAR, Stephen E. (1988)
      'Existence and Local Uniqueness of Functional Rational Expectations Equilibria in Dynamic Economic Models'
      Journal of Economic Theory, **44** (1), February: 124–55

      Spear proves the existence and local uniqueness of stationary functional RE equilibria for an open set of multi-good, multi-agent pure exchange overlapping generations models in which agents' endowments are random. He identifies them as locally isolated, functional RE equilibria; indeterminate functional RE equilibria of the Spear, Srivastava and Woodford type do not exist.

432   SPEAR, Stephen E. (1985)
'Rational Expectations in the Overlapping Generations Model'
Journal of Economic Theory, **35** (2), April 251–75

With his stochastic overlapping generations model with heterogeneous and multi-commodity markets, Spear shows that the RE equilibrium stochastic process of prices and allocations exhibits serial correlation. (In a one-commodity model an equilibrium always exists which is measure-isomorphic to the endowment process.)

433   SPEAR, Stephen E. and Sanjay SRIVASTAVA (1986)
'Markov Rational Expectations Equilibria in an Overlapping Generations Model'
Journal of Economic Theory, **38** (1), February: 35–62

The authors analyse RE equilibrium paths in a stochastic overlapping generations model. They establish the existence of non-steady-state equilibria and enumerate various stochastic properties.

434   STEGMAN, Trevor (1985)
'On the Rationality of the Rational Expectations Hypothesis'
Australian Economic Papers, **24** (45), December: 350–55

Stegman argues that the REH cannot be based soundly on principles of optimization. Neither can unbiased prediction be identified with economic rationality.

435   STOKEY, Nancy L. (1981)
'Rational Expectations and Durable Goods Pricing'
Bell Journal of Economics, **12** (1), Spring: 112–28

In her model Stokey shows that the RE equilibrium concept has no predictive value. She examines both a RE and a perfect RE equilibrium.

436   STRASSL, Wolfgang (1986)
'Keynes on Expectations and Uncertainty: Rational Expectations Equilibria with Asymmetric Information'
Bulletin of Economic Research, **38** (2), May: 137–59

Strassl considers the RE equilibrium literature. He reviews Keynes' discussion of expectations and shows how RE equilibria confirm and qualify Keynes' work.

437   STRUTHERS, John J. (1984)
'Rational Expectations: A Promising Research Program or a Case of Monetarist Fundamentalism?'
Journal of Economic Issues, **18** (4), December: 1133–54

Struthers argues that new classical economics does not encourage devastating attacks on activist government policies. He concludes that new classicism allows us to understand Friedman's theory better: it 'has completed the monetarist parable' (p. 1150).

438   SVINDLAND, Eirik (1983)
'Konjunkturtheoretische Implikationen der Hypothese rationaler Erwartungen' ('Implications of the "Rational Expectations" Hypothesis with respect to Business Cycle Theory')
Kredit und Kapital, **16** (3): 331–50

The author praises RE because actors learn from their mistakes. He indicates that the new classical version of RE clashes with the reality of business cycles.

439   SWAMY, P.A.V.B., J.R. BARTH and P.A. TINSLEY (1982)
'The Rational Expectations Approach to Economic Modelling'
Journal of Economics and Dynamic Control, **4** (2), May: 125–47

In this paper the authors suggest that conventional formulations of the REH violate the axiomatic basis of modern statistical theory by confusing 'objective' and 'subjective' notions of probability.

440 TAYLOR, John B. (1982)
'Establishing Credibility: A Rational Expectations Viewpoint'
American Economic Review: Papers and Proceedings, **72** (2), May:
81–5

In this paper Taylor considers the problem of reducing the rate of
inflation from the RE perspective in a general, nontechnical way. He
focuses on policy rules and changes in policy.

441 TAYLOR, John B. (1979)
**'Estimation and Control of a Macroeconomic Model with Rational
Expectations'**
Econometrica, **47** (5), September: 1267–86

Taylor uses a RE model to investigate the selection of macroeconomic policy rules under RE. He calculates a constant growth
rate rule for the money supply.

442 TAYLOR, John B. (1977)
**'Conditions for Unique Solutions in Stochastic Macroeconomic
Models with Rational Expectations'**
Econometrica, **45** (6), September: 1377–85

Taylor presents a simple stochastic macroeconomic model with RE
in which multiple price distribution equilibria exist even when all
unstable rational price distributions have been eliminated. Such
multiplicity results from the presence of real balances in the production function and allows random events unrelated to the economic
system to increase the variance of price levels. Taylor discusses how
multiplicity can be avoided and points out new areas for research.

443 TAYLOR, John B. (1975)
'Monetary Policy during a Transition to Rational Expectations'
Journal of Political Economy, **83** (5): 1009–21

When rational agents err in their expectations a period of learning
and adjustment will follow. Taylor examines the effects of monetary
policy during this adjustment period, concluding that such a policy
can influence real variables when inflationary expectations are in
transition.

444   TIETZEL, Manfred (1982)
**'Was kann man von der "Theorie rationaler Erwartungen" rationaler-
weise erwarten?' ('What Can Be Rationally Expected of the "Theory
of Rational Expectations"?')**
Kredit und Kapital, **15** (4): 492–516

Tietzel discusses the failings of the neutrality proposition. He argues
that the assumptions behind new classical works are unrealistic since
not all economic agents have the same expectations. On the positive
side, the theory has drawn attention to the formation of expectations.

445   TILLMANN, Georg (1985)
**'Existence and Stability of Rational Expectations Equilibria in a
Simple Overlapping Generation Model'**
Journal of Economic Theory, **36** (2), August: 333–51

Tillmann examines a simple overlapping generation model with
money (external) and one consumption good. He finds that no
model containing a learning process can reach rationality.

446   TIROLE, Jean (1982)
'On the Possibility of Speculation under Rational Expectations'
Econometrica, **50** (5), September: 1168–81

Tirole examines the case of static and dynamic speculation when
traders have RE. He argues that trading relies on inconsistent plans
– which in turn are inconsistent with RE. Integrating the RE equilibrium concept into a model of dynamic asset trading, he suggests that
more research on the manipulability of speculative markets is
required.

447   TOBIN, James (1980)
'Are New Classical Models Plausible Enough to Guide Policy?'
Journal of Money, Credit, and Banking, **12** (4), November, Part 2:
788–99

Tobin discusses the many papers that have appeared before his own.
The seeming answer to the question posed in his title is 'not really'.

448   TORR, Christopher (1984)
'Expectations and the New Classical Economics'

Australian Economic Papers, **23** (43), December: 197–205

Torr investigates RE's Ricardian roots. He argues that although Ricardians do not emphasize their importance, both they and the new classical economists treat expectations as being linked to an underlying law of motion.

449 TOWNSEND, Robert M. (1983a)
'Equilibrium Theory with Learning and Disparate Expectations: Some Issues and Methods', with comment by J.B. Taylor
in Frydman and Phelps, 1983: 169–202

In this paper the author presents an equilibrium model with learning and with disparate (but rational) expectations. He finds that the time series of these models fit the data well.

450 TOWNSEND, Robert M. (1983b)
'Forecasting the Forecasts of Others'
Journal of Political Economy, **91** (4), August: 546–88

The author investigates various linear RE equilibrium models of investment. One model he develops can handle informational structures in which decision-makers forecast the forecasts of others. Townsend argues that forecasts and forecast errors can be serially correlated.

451 TOWNSEND, Robert W. (1978)
'Market Anticipations, Rational Expectations, and Bayesian Analysis'
International Economic Review, **19** (2), June: 481–94

The author investigates the stability of (self-fulfilling) RE equilibria. He constructs consistent extended models and analyses their sequences of Nash equilibria.

452 TURNOVSKY, Stephen J. (1984)
'Rational Expectations and the Theory of Macroeconomic Policy: An Exposition of Some of the Issues'
Journal of Economic Education, **15** (1), Winter: 55–69

This is an introduction to the issues surrounding RE. The background to the development of the REH, the Lucas critique and the policy neutrality proposition are all discussed.

453   TURNOVSKY, Stephen J. (1980)
'The Choice of Monetary Instruments under Alternative Forms of Price Expectations'
Manchester School of Economics and Social Studies, **48** (1), March: 39–63

The choice of the right monetary target for stabilization purposes is the central theme of this paper. Turnovsky analyses the problem in a model subject to demand and supply shocks under rational and adaptive expectations. Supply disturbances give rise to conflict in the choice of monetary instruments, but policy is able to influence real variables.

454   TURNOVSKY, Stephen J. (1977)
'Structural Expectations and the Effectiveness of Government Policy in a Short-Run Macroeconomic Model'
American Economic Review, **67** (5), December: 851–66

Turnovsky considers a short-run macroeconomic model in which expectations of endogenous variables are rational – that is, determined by the structure of the model. He concludes, for instance, that if government wants to use a restrictive monetary policy to reduce inflation, its effectiveness will be increased if the policy is announced in advance.

455   TURNOVSKY, Stephen J. (1970)
'Empirical Evidence on the Formation of Price Expectations'
Journal of the American Statistical Association, **65** (332), December: 1441–54

The author tests models of price formation of the Korean War period determining, among other things, whether expectations conform to the REH. Some of the more recent data is found to be rational.

456   VANDERHOFF, James (1983)
'Support for Rational Expectations Models with U.S. Data'

Journal of Monetary Economics, **12** (2), August: 297–308

Vanderhoff compares the income–expenditure model, the St Louis model and the rational expectations model. He finds that the third best describes the data.

457 VERRECHIA, Robert E. (1982)
'Information Acquisition in a Noisy Rational Expectations Economy'
Econometrica, **50** (6), November: 1415–30

The author analyses a model of a competitive market in which heterogeneous traders learn both from prices and from costly information acquisition. He shows that a RE equilibrium exists in this market.

458 VISCO, Ignazio (1984)
'On Linear Models with Rational Expectations: An Addendum'
European Economic Review, **24** (1), February: 113–15

Visco shows how the method of solving linear RE models proposed by Broze and Szafarz can be made more general.

459 VISCO, Ignazio (1981)
'On the Derivation of Reduced Forms of Rational Expectations Models'
European Economic Review, **16** (2–3). June–July: 355–65

Visco shows how one can derive reduced forms of linear models containing expectations of current endogenous variables formed rationally in previous periods. He then uses this method to derive conditions for complete policy neutrality for this type of new classical model.

460 WAGNER, Helmut (1981)
'Wirtschaftspolitik im Lichte rationaler Erwartungen' ('Economic Policy and Rational Expectations')
Konjunkturpolitik, **27** (1): 1–11

Wagner discusses developments in RE theory. He then describes the area of its future application which he believes should be limited to situations of risk (in Knight's sense) and to stable systems. Thus RE theory has little relation with traditional macroeconomic areas of study.

461   WALL, Kent D. (1980)
'Generalized Expectations Modelling in Macroeconomics'
Journal of Economic Dynamics and Control, **2** (2), May: 161–84

The generalized expectations model is presented as a means of unifying economic modelling focused on expectations. Wall argues that his formulation of expectations subsumes all others as special cases. To achieve this he uses control theory – in particular Kalman filter – techniques.

462   WALLIS, Kenneth F. (1980)
'Econometric Implications of the Rational Expectations Hypothesis'
Econometrica, **48** (1), January: 49–73

Wallis considers the implications of the REH for econometrics, describing the statistical properties of these models. He argues that purely extrapolative forecasts of endogenous variables can be constructed as alternatives to RE although they are not as efficient. He also discusses the implications of RE for policy evaluation.

463   WALTERS, A.A. (1971)
'Consistent Expectations, Distributed Lags and the Quantity Theory'
Economic Journal, **81**, June: 273–81

Walters applied RE to a macro situation and gave them an improved and more sensible name – 'consistent expectations'. He is as much a founder of the RE school as are Muth, Lucas, Sargent and Wallace.

464   WASSERFALLEN, Walter (1985)
'Forecasting, Rational Expectations and the Phillips-Curve: An Empirical Investigation'
Journal of Monetary Economics, **15** (1), January: 7–27

Wasserfallen evaluates the Phillips curve using data for the Swiss economy in a RE model. He does not find a Phillips curve relationship.

465 WEDLIN, A. (1984)
'Expectations Formation and Revision in Economics'
Metroeconomica, **36** (2–3), June–October: 211–25

Wedlin considers the ideas of learning and expectations as well as the REH as a concept based on an optimizing principle. He argues that these ideas are consistent within a dynamic model incorporating the acquisition of information.

466 WEGGE, Leon L. and Mark FELDMAN (1983)
'Identifiability Criteria for Muth-Rational Expectation Models'
Journal of Econometrics, **21** (2), February: 245–54

The authors argue that, given a sufficient number of nonanticipated exogenous variables, standard rank and order conditions are sufficient to identify RE parameters.

467 WEISS, Laurence M. (1980)
'The Role for Active Monetary Policy in a Rational Expectations Model'
Journal of Political Economy, **88** (2), April: 221–33

Given exogenous (nonmarket) sources of information, Weiss' model assumes continuous market clearing and optimal forecasts of agents. The exogenous uncertainty responsible for movements in real output derives from changes in expectations of the profitability of investment. Weiss shows that such expectations need not be irrational to cause undesirable fluctuations. The model demonstrates that an active stabilization policy can have a role given rational, optimizing agents.

468 WEISSENBERGER, Edgar, Gerd MÜLLER–BROCKHAUSEN and Heinz WELSCH (1986)
'A Factor Demand Model with Quasi-fixed Factors and Rational Expectations'
Journal of Economics: Zeitschrift für Nationalökonomie, **46** (2): 123–42

The authors present a RE model of factor demand, merging RE literature with contributions to the theory of production under adjustment costs. They estimate the dynamic RE factor demand model using annual US data from the manufacturing sector. RE are rejected at the 0.05 significance level, but not at the 0.01 level.

469   WIBLE, James R. (1984–85)
'An Epistemic Critique of Rational Expectations and the Neoclassical Macroeconomic Research Program'
Journal of Post Keynesian Economics, **7** (2), Winter: 269–81

Wible criticizes RE, arguing that the theory is indistinguishable from positivism. He finds both neoclassical and RE macroeconomics very deficient.

470   WIBLE, James R. (1982–83)
'The Rational Expectations Tautologies'
Journal of Post Keynesian Economics, **5** (2), Winter: 199–207

Wible reviews the REH within the new classical tradition. He argues that the high technical level of new classical exposition makes it popular with the general public.

471   WICKENS, M.R. (1982)
'The Efficient Estimation of Econometric Models with Rational Expectations'
Review of Economic Studies, **49** (155): 55–67

Wickens argues for an errors-in-variables approach to solving RE models. As well as being easy to compute, this would guarantee consistent estimates.

472   WILLES, Mark H. (1980)
'"Rational Expectations" as a Counterrevolution'
The Public Interest, Special Edition, 1980: 81–110

Willes first discusses the RE school's criticisms of Keynesian economics and then defends RE theories.

473 WOGIN, Gillian (1980)
**'Unemployment and Monetary Policy under Rational Expectations:
Some Canadian Evidence'**
Journal of Monetary Economics, **6** (1), January: 59–68

Wogin investigates the policy implication of combining RE with the
natural rate of unemployment hypothesis by estimating a monetary
policy feedback rule for Canadian data (1927–72). The author con-
firms the hypothesis that unanticipated monetary policy has affected
unemployment in Canada, but that anticipated increases in the
money stock have not.

474 WOGLOM, Geoffrey (1982)
'Underemployment Equilibrium with Rational Expectations'
Quarterly Journal of Economics, **97** (1), February: 89–107

Woglom constructs a model in which underemployment equilibria
exist despite correct aggregate information. He argues that rational
agents may have difficulty in moving the economy away from this
underemployment equilibrium because of a free-rider problem. The
monetary authority can, however, achieve the desired equilibrium
by changing the money supply. He adds that the market structure is
not very realistic.

475 YOON, Chang-Ho (1986)
'Rational Expectations Equilibrium in a Sequence of Asset Markets'
International Economic Review, **27** (3), October: 553–64

Yoon examines the existence of a stationary equilibrium in a
sequence of asset markets. He derives a martingale property of the
stochastic equilibrium price process as a non-arbitrage condition.
Each RE equilibrium is shown to be generically revealing for a
certain class of economy.

476 YOSHIKAWA, Hiroshi (1980)
**'The Effectiveness of Monetary Policy in Two Macroeconomic
Models with Rational Expectations'**
Economic Studies Quarterly, **31** (2), August: 128–38

By comparing a new classical model with a traditional Keynesian model incorporating RE, the author finds that the policy neutrality result does not hold for the latter. One of the basic differences between the models is the flexibility of prices.

Index